Sixty Years A Que

By the same author,

WINNERS NEVER QUIT: Marguerite Rogers Howie, African American Woman Sociologist
(New Academia Publishing, 2006)

Sixty Years a Que

Gordon D. Morgan

Washington, DC

Copyright © 2010 by Gordon D. Morgan
SCARITH/New Academia Publishing, 2011

All rights reserved. No part of this book may be reproduced or transmitted in any form or by any means, electronic or mechanical, including photocopying, recording, or by any information storage and retrieval system.

Printed in the United States of America

Library of Congress Control Number: 2011924071
ISBN 978-0-9832451-4-8 paperback (alk. paper)

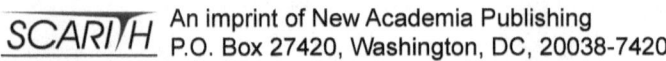 An imprint of New Academia Publishing
P.O. Box 27420, Washington, DC, 20038-7420

 info@newacademia.com - www.newacademia.com

Contents

Preface   vii
Prelude   ix

Introduction	1
1. About the Local Omegas	9
2. The Quettes	19
3. Conclaves and Assemblies	23
4. Graduate School and Later	27
5. University of Arkansas	31
Black Greeks	31
Omega Models	33
6. Cardinal Principles Examined	37
7. Tenth Anniversary Talk To Gamma Eta Chapter	45
8. Beyond Civil Rights	55
9. The Meaning of the Pledge Period	61
10. From Fun to Service	65
11. Favorites	69
12. Talking to the Deltas	75
13. Self Evaluation	77
14. Pledging Rules	85
15. Achievement Day Address	91
16. Que Finals	101
17. March of the Generations	107
Addendum I: Tribute to Lonnie Ray Williams	121
18. Back to the Beginning	123
19. Black Greek Life Today	131
The Omega Psi Phi Fraternity, Incorporated: A Script	135
Addendum II: Will My Son Pledge Omega	141

GORDON D. MORGAN, Ph.D.
Professor, University of Arkansas

Preface

    This work was begun round 1990 which would have been my 40th Anniversary as an Omega Man. I have been working on it for nearly 20 years. This year, 2009, is my 59th year as a Que. I want to thank all brothers and friends for reading it, or even mentioning it.

    Nothing about me is as good as it was when I began, including my sight and ability to find errors. I assume complete responsibility for what is said herein and for any shortcomings of the work.

Prelude

Black Fraternities and Sororities in Historical Perspective

There have been black fraternities and sororities since the early days in tribal Africa. People have long found one reason or another to cluster together on a voluntary basis, which is the foundation of brotherhood or sisterhood. Tribal Africans were initiated into fraternities based on age. They had to prove themselves worthy by undergoing hardships, running in the forests alone, being separated from their families and friends, thinking and contemplating. When they had passed these hurdles, they were given secret codes and charged with the responsibility of upholding the values for which the groups stood.

Women followed roughly the same rules. There were ceremonies, called "rites of passage," which marked off one status from another. Some of these initiation rites involved circumcision, perhaps the most widely publicized ones, because they so sharply conflicted with the values of Westerners. Jomo Kenyatta's book FACING MT. KENYA is just one of the several which describe the rites that initiates went through. In West Africa there were the Poro Societies whose initiation ceremonies have been widely described.

African societies also used what anthropologists called a classificatory system in which people in about the same status and age were bound together and had about the same relationship to each other. Oftentimes the persons entering the same status saw themselves as a special club, which we would call a fraternity or sorority.

Secret societies were prohibited during the slave period, but many did exist. Quite often these societies had as their purpose the breaking of the bonds of servitude. Slaves were united, insofar as possible through such values. Probably one of the oldest of the African fraternities which survived in the New World was based on their agreement to continue the practice of some phases of voodoo. By holding onto the old teachings around the area of religion the slaves could retain a sense of integrity and unity. So wherever a slave saw another he could be practically sure that there was a similarity, even unity, based on a belief in old African values. This belief in spirit worship might be more important than the idea that there was unity in color for not all blacks were slaves and not all slaves were black. There had been a great deal of intermixing and a color range from dark to light was soon found in the New World. Because of the failure of owners to allow unsupervised gatherings of slaves, for fear that they might foment trouble, the secret societies could not flourish openly. This did not mean that one slave would not help another. But before the Revolutionary War, Prince Hall petitioned the British Government to charter a Masonic Lodge among blacks in North America, among freemen who had previously been Masons. This lodge was probably the first recognized black fraternity in the New World. Its counterpart for women became the Eastern Star.

After the Civil War black people began to get some schooling, though a few had been given that privilege before the war. Phi Beta Kappa was the first Greek letter society established on an American campus. It was begun in 1776 at William and Mary College in Virginia. The idea that Greeks loved learning and that people who loved learning had much in common was the germ giving rise to Phi Beta Kappa. There were no academic requirements at first for membership in the association, just a willingness to learn more in the artistic and cultural fields. The atmosphere was hostile to science and so the only people who could qualify for Phi Beta Kappa were those in such fields as the liberal arts. Practical scientists then had very limited status on the campuses of America.

As more people went to college more societies sprang up. Every school had several academic societies and some for other purposes. Uniforms, grips, and other rituals were used to distinguish members. Because some of the schools of the East did not so freely practice racial discrimination a few blacks were admitted to membership in campus societies if they were otherwise qualified.

It was in the late 1890s when, following the Hayes-Tilden Compromise that segregation began to be widely practiced in the U.S.

Blacks were systematically excluded from a large variety of organizations and were forced to try to build their own societies. Some claim that Booker T. Washington helped to encourage segregation by offering his 1895 Cotton States Exposition speech during which he asserted that the races could be as separate as the fingers in regard to those things social but one as the hand in things relating to mutual progress. In the late 1890s the Sigma Pi Phi Boulé was organized, its membership comprised of black men of achievement. They wanted to provide models of success and learning so that other blacks might want to emulate them in their own achievements. The Boulé was exclusive, barring men without college degrees, holdings, material wealth, or community status. The Boulé was probably the first organization to try to make a national black group noted especially for its learning, business influence, and community standing. It was almost natural that they would encourage younger men in college to follow their example.

Greek letter societies followed the pattern of the times when nearly all institutions in America were segregated. The concept was called parallelism: blacks would establish a counterpart of all societies and clubs and actions of whites. They would develop their own society, but on the same basis of the whites. Black schools, churches, lodges, communities, businesses, and myriad other activities, banks, professions, etc., would be established and embellished. The concept today would be called apartheid. And since blacks attending the colleges above the Mason-Dixon Line would scarcely be allowed to join white societies, they would begin their own. These societies had as their purposes generally black improvement under the heading of scholarship and service, though other terms were often used. The counterpart black academic society was Alpha Kappa Mu which was said to be the black Phi Beta Kappa, admitting only the most accomplished of black students. The attempt was even to limit Alpha Kappa Mu to the same fields of study as Phi Beta Kappa.

The social fraternity movement began on white college campuses after the Civil War for the most part when there was a general expansion of youth going to college. Harvard and Yale had their Clubs which took the place of national fraternities and so did Radcliffe, Smith, Wesleyan, etc. But in the more common schools it was found that students loved these organizations and would pay to join them.

But fraternities and sororities have other functions. They help a student learn to present himself or herself better. Confidence is stressed through the pledge process, along with better social adjustment. You become better disciplined, caring more about those around you. If you are too shy, you open up more. If you are too forward and aggressive some of the steam is taken out of you. Whatever the group does is usually for the benefit of the pledge, or so it is believed.

Some say the fraternities and sororities are rating and sorting groups, helping members to find possible mates by giving them groups with whom they may relate. In years past certain fraternities paired with certain sororities, so it seemed in the public mind. Much of that has changed. One Greek is as good as another. They all stress very similar values. They stand for the student's making the most of oneself, developing a sense of humanism and appreciation for those underneath and that efforts are not forgotten to try to uplift those who need it.

During my day all Greeks had high status. We had to know the names of all Greeks on our campus regardless of whether they were affiliated with our fraternity or sorority. We had to show signatures of all Greeks on campus during our pledge period. There was believed to be a sense of harmony and brotherhood in Greekdom. No matter what colors a person wore he or she was expected to stand a little taller, be a bit more outstanding, show a little more leadership, be more highly self-motivated to use talents and resources wisely. I hope that much has not changed. I don't think it is chauvinistic to expect that Greeks provide much of the leadership on campus so that when they get out in the world this will be a natural extension of what they have been doing all along.

And I do not need to say that most Greeks have more fun than non-Greeks. Even the service projects they carry out are fun and learning experiences. Other students look up to Greeks, if they demand it by their deportment and achievement. Any fallen Greek is damaging to the whole Greek movement. So when you wear the colors remind yourself that you represent something that many others would like to find in themselves. You are a little special; you made the grades, you took the blows; you showed that you are trying to stand for something.

Several years ago I asked a particular church pastor in the black community to allow a Greek society, the Omegas, to present a public program which would have benefited the community. He said no, that the House of God was not a fitting place for Greek activities to take place. I was hurt for in more than 20 years of working with college students and Greeks there had been no separation between community and congregation and campus. We had tried for years to have at least one public program per year in the black community. This community had not seen black Greek societies and thought they behave like some of the boys and girls of the other ethnicity who are in Greek societies. The pastor, not a college man, did not know that we tried to be of benefit to the community, to serve as inspiration to the youth who have no hope. Role modeling was not invented by the present generation. But for this pastor all Greeks are the same--partying, getting in trouble, and behaving in ways unbecoming gentlemen, ladies, educated, or even sensible people. We do not need that type of image.

I had some reservations 11 years ago (when this was written the Greeks had been on this campus that many years), when the first black Greek societies were formed on the campus. I did not want black youth to get a poor reputation in the community. I did not want them to be distracted from the things of the mind. But I also realized that it is not illegitimate to be a black Greek. It is one of the many good things that we have kept alive and well over the difficult years of our transition from Africa to the more general society. I believe our organizations can compete with others, that we can attract participants of all ethnicities. On this campus (University of Arkansas) we have had at least two white members pledge and be initiated into black societies. That is a poor record but it is better than most of the white society records. Around the country there are a few members who are white in each of the black Greek societies. They are there because they found something in us which they liked and wanted to be a part of our groups. We must find something in ourselves to make us want to do the very best that we can.

On campuses today black students are not always the first of their families to go to college. Parents, one or both, may be Greek.

They want their children to become Greek. Make them proud. Get your grades together and go Greek. People will talk about you if you do and if you don't. The choice is yours. The ball is in your court. We do not apologize for being Greek. We don't have to apologize for Thurgood Marshall, U.S. Supreme Court Justice, Marva Collins, nationally known educator, Samuel Lee Kountz, world famous kidney transplant surgeon, Carter G. Woodson, Charles Wesley, Benjamin E. Mays, Jesse Jackson, dozens of world class athletes, and people of general good character who are not in the limelight. A Greek society will not make you a better person; you will have to do that yourself. But it will help you get a better handle on yourself, to become more introspective. It will encourage you to do your best, to sharpen your talent, to blame yourself for your legitimate failures, to bring you out of that shell of narrowness. Not all of you need that help, but even if you don't, you will probably be a lot better off being a Greek than not being one. (Delivered at the Delta Sigma Theta Convocation, University of Arkansas, Fall 1985).

Addendum to Prelude

When the students at the University of Arkansas, at which I teach, found that I was Greek, they wanted to know what that life was like during my time as an undergraduate. It had been nearly 20 years since my initiation in 1950 that these questions began to be asked. Twenty years was a fair length of time to be Greek. Then, I was not so hopelessly removed by age from the students. I could still relate to them. As time went on the questions continued, particularly from the newer and younger students, for others graduated and moved on to other activities in the more adult world.

I also changed and, before it, my time as an Omega Man was approaching 40 years. It was time to stop repeating the stories presented through the years and to write at least some of them down. My intention had been to pen a memoir entitled *Forty Years a Que*, which was done, but which was hidden in my cluttered files. Occasionally, students came by wanting information from more senior brothers and I would pull out the manuscript. They would look quizzically at the pictures, read a little of the prose, or just sit and talk about Greekdom then. Before I could bat my eyes, ten more years had passed and the same stories were being told. Now

I was slower of speech, grayer, more seasoned. The titled had to be changed to *Fifty Years a Que*. *It would be changed later because of the fast passage of time.*

This memoir is dedicated to the many young people who were curious about what black Greekdom was about now more than half a century ago. It is further dedicated to the memory of my son, Bryce, who followed in his father's footsteps to become an Omega legacy.

I am glad that my family and some relatives found something positive in the example I tried to set as an Omega Man. It is with great pride that I mention them and their interest and dedication to the principles on which the Omega Psi Phi Fraternity, Incorporated, was founded. In this work, materials about other fraternity members who had a big influence on my life are included. I cite especially Bro. Charles D. Henry, from my hometown of Conway, Arkansas, and my old college roommate Bro. John M. Kilimanjaro, with whom I always had a running competition. It was invigorating as well as challenging. We were the best of friends and remained so through the years. Perhaps it was the spirit of Omega that held us together in something of an unusually tight bond. Steve, as we called him, was a creative person, a writer of his own scripts. Sometimes his ideas were thought of as a little bit unusual, but that is often the characteristic of a creative and talented person. Perhaps Steve's major accomplishment was the opening and continuation over some 50 years of a community paper, *The Carolina Peacemaker*, in Greensboro, North Carolina.

When the children were growing up we tried to have them associate with persons who were considered as "going somewhere." This did not mean they could not associate with children of all social descriptions and categories. If there is anything we detested, it was the snobbishness of false social class. It was not easy for college professors' children to grow up. The little differences that we had in terms of homes, automobiles, and other status symbols were not sufficient to place us in another category. But there was a difference in perceptions of people toward people who had advanced degrees. While they might not have had the money, the learning they were assumed to have was enough sometimes to cause others to stand back off them.

The boys were pretty good friend-makers. They engaged in the rough and tumble with children of all classes. They could mix with the high and the low and recognized no basic differences between any of them. They were not good athletes but they could carry their part. They were runners, not really outstanding, but they were pretty good. And they held down some of the back chairs in strings. They were pretty fair students overall. The main thing was that they tried to develop winning personalities, to be friends to all, to take their lumps without crying.

The girls were more withdrawn. Maybe it was harder for girls to grow up than boys. The reins on them were a lot tighter, but they imposed some on themselves. Their early achievements in schools were not as notable as the boys. But that did not matter much to us.

We tried to instill in the children the meanings of things we did when we were much younger. As our parents told us of their elementary school days--that was the limit of their schooling—we told our children of our days at the various levels of schooling. When they were small we told them of the exciting days we had in grammar and junior high school. I was particularly pleased to tell them how I cried the first time I was to kiss a girl in a part in elementary school. My mother still has the little tuxedo they made out of very thin cloth for me to wear in the school play. They learned all about our spelling bees, our attempts at playing sports, tricks on teachers. We couldn't believe that a 32 mile bus ride to Little Rock when we were growing up was a two hour affair and that one day on my first ever trip to Little Rock, a school outing to the zoo, I was given 15 cents for my lunch and dinner. I would not spend a cent, even after some heavy prodding by my teacher, Mrs. Hill. Needless to say, I was a very hungry child when we reached home in the late afternoon.

As they got older and Omega men came around, we introduced them. I told them about these men being brothers. Of course that encouraged them to want to know what we meant. There were symbols displayed around the house which caught their attention as they grew up.

Our older son was 15 when we began a chapter of Omega Psi Phi on the campus of the University of Arkansas. The younger boy was eight. There were Omega men in and out of the house fairly frequently. My brother-in-law, my blood brother in California, and some of their friends, as well as faculty members at the campus were at the house often enough to impress upon the boys what Omega meant. At that age they were somewhat encouraged by some of the visitors to consider Omega when they were ready.

In an effort to widen our own knowledge and theirs too, we traveled fairly often. We drove to Mexico City just before the 1968 Olympics. But one year we went to Washington, D.C. A highlight of that visit was to Howard University to see the shrine of the Omegas. The boys were still pretty young but I am glad that made an impact on them.

After my older son had been in college for a year he decided to join a pledge line. His line was discontinued by order of the National Office after a pledge was killed in initiation rituals. That son joined the Air Force after graduation and will probably complete his initiation when he has a chance to do so. It was my younger son who most internalized the meaning of the fraternity. I fondly recall one year that the chapter was having some sort of function in a downtown hotel. My wife and I were at the head table. Somewhere through the deliberations we saw our youngster casually stroll into the meeting, come up to the table and ask us for something, I don't recall what it was. But he was very impressed with whatever the Omegas were doing. I had no idea at the time that he would become a great believer in the fraternity.

Introduction

When I joined the fraternity in 1950, it wasn't yet forty years old. No brother could write a history of 40 years, although longer periods of history were anticipated. The fiftieth anniversary of my own membership in the fraternity coincides with the year 2000, the opening of the new century. I do not know how many other brothers will write their impressions of the history of the fraternity so that younger brothers will have a sense of its history. Perhaps they will understand that they do not make the fraternity, nor will their achievements, or lack of them, break it. Omega Psi Phi Fraternity will rise or fall to the extent it continues to address the brotherhood needs of young men wherever they are found.

It has been a long time ago that I was initiated and all the rituals and ceremonies have been substantially altered. New brothers are coming into the fraternity with new ideas of what it is like, of what brotherhood means. There are now as many as three or four generations of Omegas in some families. The tradition is firmly established in many. Two generations of brothers are no longer uncommon. I was happy when my older son decided to follow in the footsteps of his father and three other uncles into the fraternity. His line was stopped for reasons over which he had no control. He has not yet completed his initiation. I hope he is like Bill Cosby and decides to complete it before he reaches too far into middle age or before I am too feeble to appreciate it.

It was a special treat when my younger son, now late, decided to pledge Omega. He completed the process, enjoyed the fraternization with other young men, and was enjoying what the fraternity could offer him and what he could offer it, before his passing.

Fifty years is a long way to look back. Much has happened. I want to tell young brothers what the fraternity was like when I was a young initiate. I know my experiences are not to be taken as wholly representative for there were differences on each campus. The college, Arkansas Agricultural, Mechanical and Normal College (Hereafter AM&N College) was on the quarter system then. It began the fall term in early September. I entered in 1949 as a rather undistinguished freshman, although I held a valedictorian scholarship where I was first in a class of fifteen. I was not the smartest student. The smartest ones seemed to have dropped out. By the time I was ready to complete high school, the school had been offering high school diplomas for only about ten years. High school graduate was still a big thing, and college attendance was even bigger. A family whose children went to college, any college, was expected to carry themselves a little higher than those whose children did not go. It was not necessary to go immediately following graduation, but if you could manage it, so much the better. Because of economic restrictions, and the absence of opportunity for scholarships, not many young people went to college. The enrollment at AM&N College, during the year I enrolled, was 1100 students, by far the largest enrollment in the history of the institution that began in 1875.

There were two dormitories for boys and two for girls (as youth were called then, with no sense of diminution of status), a home economics building, a Smith–Hughes building, a gymnasium, a laundry, and not much else. One of the big freedoms we enjoyed was going to the laundry on Saturday morning to get our clothes. Needless to say, some of them were lost during the several days we had to wait for them to be laundered. We took our meals in an old military barracks and were happy to stand outside in the rain and cold weather while waiting to get into the cafeteria. Numbers were given out but that did not keep a lot of line–cutting, pushing, and shoving, and other shenanigans from taking place. From time to time there was not enough food in the dining hall to feed the students. Seconds were almost unheard of. Powdered eggs and grits were common for breakfast and occasionally a glass of milk or orange juice.

There had been a graduate chapter on the campus for some time when I enrolled. It was begun by the president of the college.

The graduate chapter was about three years old when I pledged. By 1948 initiations had been going on for about three years at the most and the initiates were mostly former soldiers from World War II. They had the grades, the leadership skills, and the money and so not all that many younger students were members. As the war years receded into the background, the average age of students fell and 18 year olds began to be more prominent on the campus.

Because other fraternities were also coming on campus, the competition for members began to pick up. Although one could not pledge before the opening of the sophomore year, students were beginning to be looked at during their first terms on campus. Administrators did not want students to let anything interfere with their studies. They understood the struggles of even the affluent parents to educate their children, as well as the roles the youth would play in offering encouragement to the people of their communities who were facing both poverty and discrimination. Since Greek membership meant much more then as a sign of success, some youth who became Greeks were tempted to cease their studies or even drop out of college. Moreover, enrollment was needed to convince legislators and funding sources that more teachers, facilities, buildings, and services were needed at the campus.

The first thing looked for were grade point averages. The groups competed strongly to see which had the higher averages as these averages were put on the campus bulletin board for all to see, including the names and averages of student members. It was more embarrassing to have your group at the bottom of the list in terms of grade point averages than to be dismissed from the campus. There was also concern with whether candidates showed conventional moralities, and especially toward the opposite sex. All groups were especially hard on persons with unusual sex orientations and most would not consider them for membership.

Students had some idea of which way they wanted to go when they reached the campus and began to engage in studies and activities in order to prove to the group in which they were interested, that they were both worthy and eligible. At the end of the first term, the grades were posted for all students on the bulletin board. The Honor Roll and Delinquent List held the most interest. The fraternities and sororities began to look at the Honor Roll and to encourage those students in their direction. Sometimes the courting of high average students was most undisguised.

Since the typical group required a C+ average for selection, one struggled to at least get that average. Sometimes the easier courses were taken as insurance that the average could be gained. Professors such as Garland Kyle, Rufus Caine, Tilman Cothran, Butler Henderson, and Elbert Tatum, were avoided as long as possible so that grade point averages would not plummet below the level of eligibility for Greek pledging.

Oftentimes a C+ average was not enough and some groups such as the Alpha Kappa Alpha sorority expected candidates to post B averages for consideration. A person could, however, have other compensating qualities. If a student were captain of a team, a distinguished soloist, pianist, debater, stage-crafter, or other person active on the campus, a C+ might be good enough. Some groups took people who could not get into the group they wanted

Those getting their second choice groups were sometimes thought of as lukewarm. Sometimes students with good averages were not all that highly sought because they did not present the image their group wanted to portray. Most groups wanted to attract people who could cut the mustard both socially and academically. We had to write a letter to the Dean of Pledges telling all about ourselves and why we wanted to join the fraternity. Once the letter was written it became common knowledge on the campus and students began to exhibit a different attitude toward the candidate. If one wrote a letter to one group, it was tantamount to being blackballed by all other groups. It was important to make up one one's mind the first trip around. Sometimes it was completely unexpected that a person was even thinking of going a certain way. For others the choice was foreclosed. When people did not go the way expected, there was usually some discussion. In homes hard feelings have come up because people went the wrong way.

After we were scrutinized through our letters, a pledge club was formed and the process leading to initiation begun. The period of preparation was roughly eight weeks, though some big brothers frightened us into believing it could be for the entire year. Some cited pledges who had been in process for years, claiming they had not exhibited the proper attitude toward the fraternity.

What happened to us would be called hazing. We called it fun and decided we would get even with the next group when we were initiated.

The roughest thing that happened to me and my group was the wiping of smiles off one's face. For smiling a brother could drag his hand over a pledge's face. No scars were left, thought there would be great gesturing and contorting of bodies by the big brother as he prepared to wipe a smile off the face of a pledge. Hilarious jokes were told in the presence of the little brother with express prohibitions against their smiling. Some of those jokes were so funny they would make Buddha laugh and it was just too hard to hold it in.

Sometimes when a "big brother" was sad, he might require a pledge club to launch into song. They were thoroughly upbraided for not sounding good as they sang. This forced them to practice together at off hours so that they could satisfy the brothers.

Shoe shining was a chore that "little brothers" got a lot of. It seemed like every "big brother's" shoes needed polishing. Since fraternity members were generally upper classmen, they lived in different dormitories. Underclass pledges could be seen carrying shoes to and from their dormitories, sometimes at a trot. Pledge club meeting was usually once per week, but as initiation time neared meetings could be more frequent. Pledge Club work consisted of learning a lot of Greek symbolism, and the history and lore of the fraternity.

During the week of initiation, we were expected to wear different costumes, generally suits, with turbans as headdress. We carried purple and gold lanterns and were expected to maintain strict silence, except in the presence of teachers, our employers, or other authority figures. During Hell Week we were expected to eat square meals, meaning that utensils had to be handled at right angles. All Greeks were to be addressed as Most Noble Greek Big Brother was to prefix the name of any Omega man. To appreciate other Greeks we had to learn the hymns of several. These, in addition to our own. Some brothers required that pledges call them Most Noble Greek Big Brother (First, Middle, and Last Name). In my case I would address my own brother, then a fraternity member, as Most Noble Greek Thomas Cephas Morgan. We tried not to get together during the pledge period because we did not want to go through the ritual.

One was not a brother until the final initiation and there were strict rules against even acting like one wanted to wear the symbols or even the colors before initiation. The formal initiation was conducted around nightfall in our area. It was a welcome relief for we had been preparing for it for quite some weeks. The last week of the initiation was called Hell Week because we were expected to literally and figuratively go through hell in exhibiting our determination to become good members. The day the Omegas were to come off was one the campus noticed. It was a different day, hushed, solemn, people waiting for the final public ceremony, a march around the campus in tuxedos, carrying lighted torches, and humming Omega Dear. We were then marched to the college farm, or to some other vacant building out of the way, where we underwent the ritual. When we finished we went back to the campus in a group, full of enthusiasm and love for all Omegas wherever they were. It was a great bonding experience. Our girlfriends were waiting for us at the campus. If we did not have a girlfriend, one came up and took our arm. They cried and laughed and hugged us and for a while there were no problems in the world. We had a meal at the Elite Grill or at the Lion's Den. Later that evening we serenaded the campus with the girls hanging out of their dormitory windows listening, crying, and some occasionally shouting, as is done is some churches. By midnight we dropped into bed but rose early the next morning, to dress up—shirt, tie, and coat, polished shoes—sporting our new pins. Occasionally, we borrowed the sweater of another brother (We would never anticipate making Omega by purchasing a sweater in advance) and styled out happy that we were now men–even real men.

After initiation, things often started to change for us. The most general change was our own growth in confidence. Now we thought that there were no limits to what we could achieve. Where we thought earlier that we did not have much promise, after initiation we ere sure that the sky was indeed the limit. It was a wonderful, euphoric feeling. I do not know how long that feeling lasted, but I think it held on for quite a while.

After the euphoria wore off, and reality settled down upon us, we tried hard to live up to the principles of the fraternity. We submerged our own personalities, in some respects, and extended or modified in other ways. For some the change was more noticeable than in others. Friends could date certain of our behavior from before initiation and after initiation. For the majority of brothers, we believe the change was positive. We did our projects and fraternized a lot together, but tried not to become clannish. Most of us cherished our friendship with members who were not of our fraternity. I had lots of friends who were members of Alpha Phi Alpha. The Kappa Alpha Psi fellows were kidded as being those who couldn't make Omega. It was all in fun. We discovered that for real friends, different fraternity membership did not get in the way.

When we were ready to graduate, it was time to move into the real world. That sometimes meant cutting the ties to the fraternity because so many of the communities where we landed to work did not have college people and there were no chapters. It was costly to go a hundred miles often in a round trip to attend meetings. The fraternities had a better chance of having graduate chapters in the larger cities in which most of the activities were sponsored. A lot of the activities were sponsored on the campus, however. After a few years away from the campus, young brothers were as surprised as others to know that some of us were Omegas for there was often no way of identifying with the group in the locations where we found ourselves. The fraternity nevertheless continued to mean a lot to most of us and we were always happy to identify with those brothers who were into positive things and making a difference.

A sense of brotherhood continued to prevail among brothers long after our college days. It was always a good feeling to be pointed out by younger brothers that we were trying to uphold the values of the fraternity. That they wanted to identify with us was always a positive. As we moved through life, friendship became more important than what fraternity symbols one wore, though it was good to know that one could find friendship in his own group. There remained friendly competition among members of the different Greek societies, but nothing that was rancorous or destructive.

During the almost fifty years of my membership in the fraternity, I must say that it has been positive for me. The friends I have made through being identified with the group; the acceptance by other fraternity members whom I had never seen, made it all worth it. I cannot say that I have been financial all those years, but I have many of them. Sometimes I was too far removed from a chapter and joined the detached chapter. This option allowed a member to continue to support the fraternity, to be identified with its programs, even though there was no local chapter with which to affiliate.

But perhaps I should begin at the beginning. This story is not everywhere in chronological sequence. These notes have been recorded over a number of years.

1

About the Local Omegas

Tau Sigma Chapter had been on the campus since about 1946, by the time I became a freshman in 1949. The picture seen in this section was taken from a 1948 yearbook. Many of the brothers joined the chapter after military service. Indeed, quite a few of the males at the college were returning veterans. They looked mature to 17 and 18 year olds and naturally we looked up to them. They had taken a few years out of their school or work programs to fight in World War II. At their return they gave a particular character and flavor to the chapter and to the campus. Veterans had a big effect on the campus at large.

In the first few years the veterans were back they practically took over the student activities on campus. They could easily get elected as student government officers as well as officers within the numerous clubs which were being formed on campus.

On the next page are pictures that we present sentimentally, but they help us to better understand the impact of the Greeks on the campus. In the first picture, from left to right, bottom row, are Elihu Gaylord, later a minister and head of the NAACP in Arkansas. The other two persons to his left I cannot identify, but they were veterans. To the right of the Shield is Nelson Talbot outstanding later in chapter work in Los Angeles. Fred Balenton, from my hometown of Conway, Arkansas, is next. Harmon Hill is to the left of Balenton. He was from El Dorado, as I remember, and was very oustanding in various campus activities. I remember Hill as being the announcement man for the choir's weekly radio program arranged through a Little Rock station. I think he was also the color man for the football games.

The first two brothers on the second row I cannot identify but I heard they were outstanding students. Third from left is Willie E. Fowler who later received the M.D. degree at Meharry or Howard Medical School. Fowler was Dean of Pledgees during my pledge period and a hard but fair one he was. Next is Willie McCree who received his doctoral degree from the University of Arkansas and became an outstanding professor at Texas Southern University. Edward Mays was a brilliant student, graduating with high honors, as did McCree. Mays completed some 20 years in the military service as a medical doctor. He was one of he early black enrollees in the University of Arkansas Medical School, about the third, I believe. The first was Edith Irby who married Bro. James B. Jones, prominent educator and university administrator in Arkansas and Texas. Mays left the service as a Colonel and later served on the staff at Meharry Medical College in Nashville, Tennessee. Thomas Baskins has been involved with farm demonstration work in Arkansas for years. He came from Morrilton, Arkansas. Presently, he is very much active in the AM&N College Alumni Association. His brother, now Dr. Lewis Baskins, joined the fraternity in the early 1950s. I do not recognize the brothers to the left of Baskins.

Time has dimmed my memory of the first brother, third row left. The second was James Davis who became an agricultural extension man in Eastern Arkansas. The names of the next four brothers escape me. The seventh is James T. Jones, I believe. He was once president of the student government at the college. He became professor of political science at Atlanta University. Jones was regarded as a very brilliant student. The next three brothers I do not know.

More than three-fourths of the brothers were former servicemen. Their maturity made them role models for the rest of the students for some years to come.

We were very happy to talk about the achievements of some of the brothers. One of our favorites was Brother Lawrence A. Davis, president of the college. Brother Davis, whom we would not call brother publicly, out of deference to his position, instead called him Prexy or Dr. Davis. President Davis had just returned to the campus from negotiating with North Central Association personnel trying to persuade them to give accreditation to the college so that credits earned at AM&N would be respected and honored. To Davis' right is Bro. Earl Ford, a very able biology professor at the institution.

In the next picture, from left to right are Brother Davis and Brother Charles Hicks, then Superintendent of education for blacks in Arkansas. Next is Alphaman Dr. Garland Kyle, prominent mathematician who later became Dean of Instruction at AM&N. The other instructor escapes me, but I think he had something to do with the program in mechanic arts.

The first full picture is of Brother John M. Howard, then head of the department of art. Bro. Howard was an accomplished and highly recognized artist in his own right. At one time he roomed in Harlem with Bro. Langston Hughes. For years Bro. Howard was a fixture in public relations, including preparing the campus and city for homecoming and other activities. He wrote news releases and otherwise publicized the work going on at the college.

Brother Ariel M. Lovelace was special to everyone on the campus. He was highly noted for his work with the choir. Lovelace was a very considerate taskmaster whose competence made us all respect him highly. He seemed to have taken some interest in me. I do not know why he let me make the traveling choir in 1949. I was not an outstanding or trained musician. I am glad to have had some acquaintance with him. I hear that from all he taught over his long career.

Being a member of a fraternity provided an opportunity to find out things about oneself, things which he did not know, to uncover talent, to gain self-confidence. I stress these things because they were important to me. Perhaps other people did not need them as much as I. Both my pledge club and my chapter were relatively small. There were only four in the pledge club. Graduation and other circumstances usually depleted the ranks of the regular chapter by anywhere from a third to a fourth of it membership. We were in pretty good shape if we maintained a membership of 15 brothers throughout a year.

But whether there were ten or twenty, the group was so diverse, the number of personalities so outstanding that getting along with them all and finding something to appreciate in each brother, however different he was from the ideal, or even the rest of us was a feat not to go unnoticed. One of the biggest learning then was that people are different, even within the same family. Try as we might there was no way of remaking a brother to fit our preset molds. That was hard for some of the brothers to understand. Because of the peculiarities of pledging, sometimes there were groups of guys who wanted to go over as a group. Ir. they were athletes they might for a few semesters project the image that the chapter was biased toward athletes. Occasionally, a group of aspiring scholars came together in the pledge club. And each chapter was happy to note that pledges of high grade point average were choosing the fraternity. In that case the group might become known as eggheads, or academic heavyweights. The character of the chapter changed constantly, but it went on through the years.

Learning to get along with a variety of people, from different academic and social circumstances, and even gaining their confidence to the extent that they could elect one to represent them as a leader, was one of the most important lessons, which the fraternity helped teach. Running those weekly and special meetings when there were those who wanted to go in different directions, trying to keep up the morals of the group, trying to elicit cooperation so that the group would look good in some sort of project it was carrying out all required negotiation, give and take, consideration of others while fighting hard for what one thought was right. We had meetings in which the brothers literally knocked down and dragged out each other but before leaving we tried to form a circle, sing the hymn and leave with our hearts full of love and appreciation for our brothers, absent the fact that some were still a little misguided, according to our individual perceptions. Not holding grudges was well taught from our perceptions for we thought that brotherhood overrode those differences separating us. So any brother, however nondescript, could feel as comfortable with the biggest athletic star, or the brother who was a member of Alpha Kappa Mu Scholastic Honorary. Brotherhood served to erase differences.

And from that appreciation for other brothers we learned more of appreciation for self. Some of us arrived in college with egos battered because of home circumstance, or difficulties in paying one's bills in school, or a number of other things. We might have had problems with making grades. From a variety of corners there were assaults on our self concepts, but the group helped us to overcome those limitations. We found in the group people with the same problems, or often they were worse than ours. How to share was learned, not only the few physical pleasures we were fortunate enough to have, but to share psychologically with those who needed it. Sometimes a fraternity brother was the only person around you felt like confiding in, or he or they in you.

When a brother had learned to respect himself, to really feel comfortable with himself, he was ready to feel comfortable with and respect others, his brothers as well as members of other fraternities and sororities. Membership in the fraternity was a way of widening one's circle of appreciation. The give and take which was necessary in the chapter, was a small sample of that which would be necessary in the larger more diverse world. The other Greek chapters represented part of that diversity. Although the Alphas, Kappas, and Sigmas were touted as being greatly different from the Omegas, we learned to negotiate those imputed differences, to feel comfortable with them, or any other Greeks. There was a fairly strong bond of appreciation between the Greeks promoted largely, though not exclusively, through the Panhellenic Council.

It was some years after leaving the campus that I became fully aware of why prospective employers wanted to know what your activities were in college. Writing a Greek affiliation on a vita sheet was sometimes thought to be a request for special help, if it were known that a brother, or someone sympathetic was in the hiring role. There were those who wanted to capitalize on their Greek connections. But I believe the main reason that affiliation was important was that it signaled to employers that here was a person who had a particular kind of social experience which helped prepare him or her to function in a group wider than his or her own. To become a Greek member usually meant that one had pretty fair grades, was able to good-naturedly take the status reduction required in pledging; some call it hazing, and to emerge generally with improved self-confidence. There was no better evidence of at least the verbal commitment to values that are thought of as progressive. A Greek was something like an Eagle Scout. One had to go through a considerable number of different trials to get it and if one survived it told something of that person's basic character.

The blackball was one of the basic screening tools a chapter had at its command. No member was obligated to vote for any person. I am happy to say that during the nearly 60 years that I have been affiliated with the fraternity, I never saw a need to cast a blackball. Usually the selection process was such that persons not thoroughly committed to becoming Greeks were excluded. The grade point average stopped the majority. Keeping one's head to the books long enough to get the required average and a little over for insurance, was sufficient incentive for many. Unfortunately the grades of too many dropped after they were initiated giving the impression that going Greek had gone to their heads. In fact, it could be the other way around. The rewards of higher education my not be as high as the perceived rewards of going Greek, on the other side the individual would study just as hard after becoming Greek as before. I believe the results teach that if the reward is valued highly enough the individual will put out the effort to reach the goal. But there is a lot of evidence that higher education, at least for black folks, does not always mean bigger rewards. In fact, one could be penalized for scholastic excellence. There are many cases of black Ph.D.'s serving as Red Caps at the old railway stations in the big cities, of lawyers barely making enough money to keep their shops open, of doctors who had to hold self and status together by collecting money from rental property for there was no room in the hospital for them to practice, often because of racism.

The fraternity revolved around a number of activities in competition with other Greek societies on campus. The campus itself was the center of the Pine Bluff African American community. Those persons who had aspirations of upward mobility used the campus as their model. Nearly all of the community thought that the campus represented the highest aspirations and achievements of those who were in the area. Downtown people who ran stores were a little more concerned with the campus and tended to cater to it to the extent possible.

Students were somewhat special and could be depended upon to deport themselves well and to make no trouble for the people of the city. Students had not become politicized by this time. Although the idea of service was present, service did not mean what it does today. Service was confined largely to the campus. The Greeks could serve as sponsors of certain activities. They could host important persons who came to town and be role models for the rest of the campus.

TAU SIGMA CHAPTER BROTHERS--Late 1940s

Davis and School Leaders--Circa 1940

16   *Sixty Years A Que*

Bro. John M. Howard, noted artist.

Bro. Ariel M. Lovelace, ALM6N College Choral Director.

About the Local Omegas   17

Bro. Morgan and dates at formal.

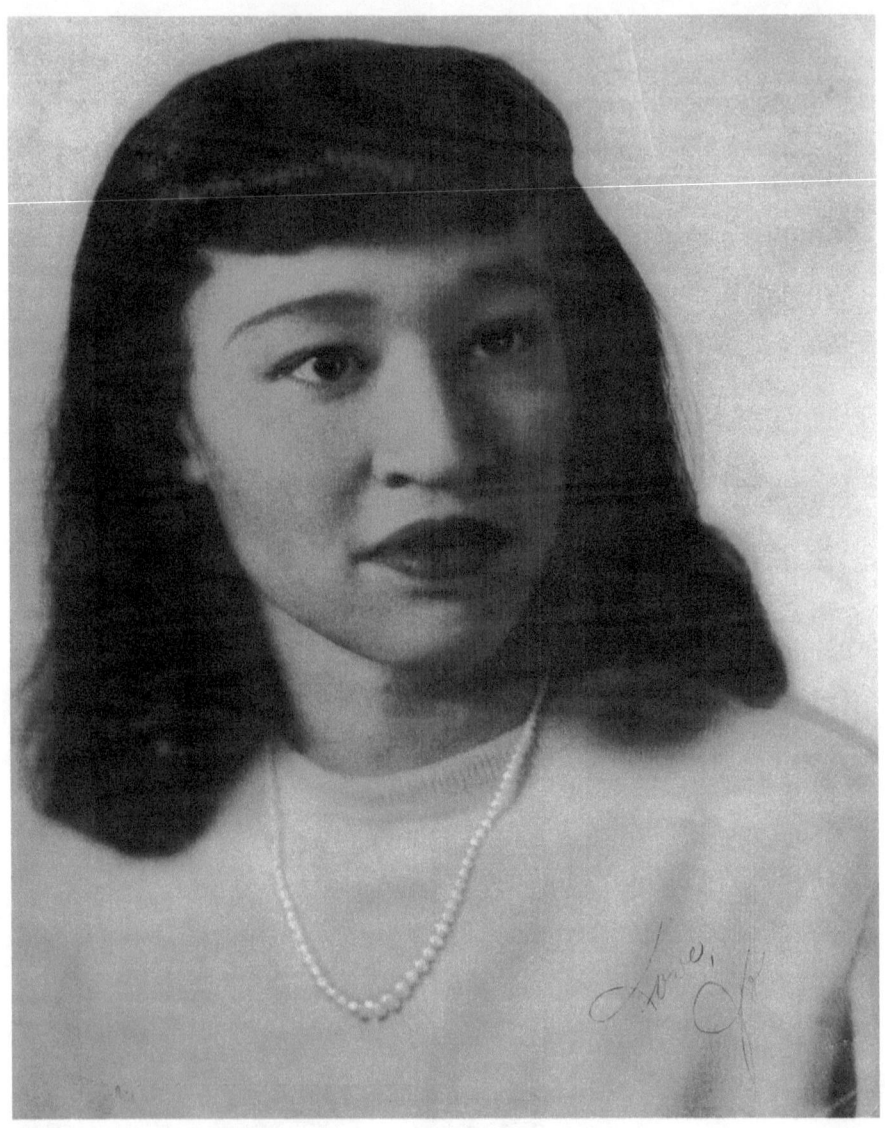

Miss Josephine Anderson. She loved Ques.

2

The Quettes

One of the things I noticed about the fraternity, or at least in the several chapters I have had the privilege of being associated with, was that ladies enjoyed the Omegas almost as much as the guys themselves. On the campus there were girls whose preferences were Omegas almost to the exclusion of men of other fraternities. Just why this was the case I do not know. Maybe there were girls who felt the same way about Alpha Phi Alphas, Kappa Alpha Psi's, and Phi Beta Sigmas. There were several important dances on campus each year and they were invitational. Girls more or less waited to see if they could be given bids to attend the dances. For the girl going to the dance was a sign that she had some recognition and status on the campus. And since not all girls could go, the ones who were invited felt they were a little bit special.

All the male Greek organizations sponsored annual balls, if their brothers paid their assessments or raised money for the function in other ways. The balls were all colorful and required elaborate preparations. Back in the early 1950s the dances were held in the Old Gymnasium which was decorated with pine fronds, paper streamers, and balloons. All Greeks were generally invited to all balls but single members were discouraged from attending. This meant that even though the sororities were invited the girls needed dates. Most often the dates came from the ranks of the Greeks. But often there were non-Greeks in attendance, particularly those who garnered enough independent popularity to be seriously considered by attending Greeks.

Someone was generally on hand to take pictures of the guys in their tuxedos and the girls in their evening gowns. I made several balls and have kept some of the pictures that were made. I don't know who the girls are. Time has dimmed my memory. But they were my dates at the time. We did not keep in contact over the years. But, I remember, those were very enjoyable times. And, honestly, the campus might have come to a halt at least during the few days preceding the balls. The gym had to be decorated which meant that students had to be excused from classes to do it, though they were dismissed for other reasons. Often we worked late into the night to get the gym in shape. The girls had to make their gowns, or find someone who would make them for they ordinarily did not have enough money to purchase new ones, though some did. Sometimes someone had to go to work for a few days in order to earn the money to afford tuxedos and corsages which the girls were expected to wear. How would the group know that a girl was with a Que unless she had the symbols fixed into her corsage? Little fuzz-covered pieces of wire of the fraternity colors bent into the appropriate Greek symbols and worked into the corsage served the purpose well enough. As I remember a corsage cost about $3.00. And there was a little discreet drinking during the dances. A guy had to have a little jug in his coat pocket, just for respect.

But it was not simply that the girls wanted to go to the Omega Ball, which generally proved to be one of the best and best attended by campus and town dignitaries. There were some courtships and marriages across such as Omega-Delta and Alpha-AKA lines. The ties were not quite as tight between the Kappa men and Sigma Gamma Rho women as they were between the previous two sets of groups, but the Phi Beta Sigmas and Zeta Phi Betas were pretty tight, from what I could observe. In communities where there were enough brothers to form a chapter there were women who formed groups called the Quettes. Generally, they were married to Omega men, but sometimes they were not. They just enjoyed the association of Omega men and the organization was a convenient one for them. The Quettes had regular meetings and fraternized by sponsoring teas, book reviews, showers for brides or new mothers, etc. They enjoyed the association with other women who had some ties to Omega men. In one town the Quettes took it upon themselves to see that the Omegas had uniform smoking jackets for an important ball. And the women cut across Greek lines. If a wife or girlfriend were not a member of a group traditionally associated with the Omegas, that was alright. The critical thing was that she liked the Omegas and cherished some connection to them. Within the Quette group her own Greek affiliation was relatively underplayed. And some of the ladies were not exactly spring chickens. They had enjoyed fellowshipping with the Omegas and the women who liked them for many years. It was fascinating just to think about what they saw in the Omegas. Evidently they saw something they liked.

Things changed, however, throughout the years. At one time women took the status of their husbands. A woman was happy to be married to a Que, in the instant case. And we know of quite a few cases where the women were not satisfied until their husbands or boyfriends had been initiated into the Omegas.

But today it is different. The Quettes are not as visible as they were in the past. Probably this is due to the influence of the Womens Liberation Movement which sought to place the woman on a level of parity with the man. She had her career and he had his. Her status became independent of his. In some cases she might not even take his name.

Another factor eroding the interest of the women in auxiliaries such as the Quettes was the changing of the organization from primarily academic and social to service. Now a woman does not need a connection to a male in order to operate in a service. club. Organizations such as the Rotary International, Kiwanis Clubs, and Chambers of Commerce have all admitted women as members and even some challenges have been made to collegiate Greek societies to cease limitations of membership based on gender.

3

Conclaves and Assemblies

The fraternity is bureaucratically organized. The country is divided into districts. There are ten districts covering the U.S. and chapters in Africa and the West Indies. It seems that the bulk of the chapters and members are in the southeastern part of the U.S. These are the states of the Old South. They are fewer in other parts but nevertheless significant. There are state, regional, and national meetings. The annual or periodic meetings are called conclaves and presided over by a basileus. The other officers, in addition to the Basileus, are respectively, vice-basileus, Keeper of Records and Seals (secretary), Keeper of Finance (treasurer), Keeper of Peace (sergeant at arms), and Chaplain. The Editor of the *Oracle*, the Official Organ of the fraternity, is an important individual who has much to say about the general publicity of the fraternity through its quarterly journal. Each officer has a vice, if the numbers warrant. At the national level the operating chief of the fraternity is the Executive Secretary, who has a staff in Washington, D.C. There is an elected board to which the Executive Secretary reports. At the lower levels the officers correspond to those named. The fraternity headquartes shifted to Atlanta.

It is at the regional and national conclaves that one can see the more public meaning of the fraternity. There are individuals in each region who have not missed meetings in many years. The fraternity is their principal concern and they are very religious about it. At the national level, in particular, the Grand Basileus and Executive Secretary have important political connections. The Black Greek heads represent about 10% of the black voting population, making them a significant block. They are given full billing by the political leaders in Washington especially. In regions or states where the Greeks are strong the leaders have corresponding political influence. Consequently there is quite a contest among individuals to become Grand Basileus. It means the individual must be highly presentable on a national level for that head will be sought out for opinions on various matters affecting blacks. Because there are many chapters throughout the country and abroad, the Grand Basileus of the Omegas will be sought out to make speeches almost constantly at college campuses, at Founders Day occasions and at a large variety of other functions. The national head of a black Greek organization, especially the old ones, will be invited to most of the important social events in the city in which he or she lives. These offices require hard work and physical stamina, but they do have their psychological payoffs. It does not hurt one's image or vita sheet to be able to list election to a high national black Greek letter organization.

The first time I attended a regional meeting was in 1959 or 1960. It was held in Houston's YMCA. There were norms at work with which I was not familiar. Two things impressed me very much at that meeting. The first was the age of the brothers present. They were generally mature and took the work of the fraternity seriously. I cannot recall what the agenda was, but it was organized around meeting the four cardinal principles of the fraternity: manhood, perseverance, scholarship and uplift. We had to drive from Pine Bluff, Arkansas to Houston, a distance of about 500 miles. There were no hotels or motels to stay in en route. We had to drive continuously, and we did so in shifts. We arrived a few minutes late and upon trying to enter the meeting were told that we had to pay $1 for being late.

Being imbued, as I was then, with the idea of brotherhood, and not wanting to pay the $1, when I finally got the floor, I complained strongly about this imposition, of how inconsiderate it was of the leadership to charge brothers who had made a special commitment to get to the meeting, involving hardship and considerable cost. My complaint was to naught. Some brother who had been attending for years, spoke after me, and instructed the chair to inform the brother, myself, that had I been attending the meetings I would have known that the $1 rule for lateness to meetings had been in effect for quite some years. The next thing that impressed me was a 90 year old brother, an Episcopal priest, who was honored. He hobbled to the podium, almost whispered through his unprepared speech for a few minutes during which he said, as he was about to close, "Oh how good it is for brothers to dwell together..." after which the group broke into thunderous applause, thinking the aged brother was finished. The old brother feebly raised his hand for quiet. The group immediately honored his gesture and stillness settled over the audience of a couple of hundred men. The old brother completed his speech with two final words, "in peace."

I have not forgotten that old brother's suggestion. He plainly implied that brothers may dwell together in a variety of unwholesome relationships, but he stressed that they dwell together in peace. I say that today to myself, and occasionally to audiences to which I speak. "How good it is for people of all identities, ethnicities, orientations, persuasions, to dwell together in peace."

Attending a Grand Conclave had been one of my ambitions when I was much younger, but I could never seem to afford it. It was hard to get connected with a chapter which would help raise the money to send a representative to the conclave. We did once or twice at the undergraduate level, however. It was the same for attendance at the regional conclaves. This conclave, held sometimes in the early 1970s, I think, was also in Houston. By that time I was interested in having the children see black people who were tryng to make a difference in their communities and in the world. The Omegas, as had the main fraternities and sororities, had begun scheduling their national meetings by then in the largest hotels in the largest cities. This time one of the biggest and classiest hotels in Houston was the meeting place of the conclave. We could not afford room in that hotel but opted for the more economical one across the street, so to speak. I think it was something like a Holiday Inn.

It was after sundown. We had seen some of the sights of Houston but had been very impressed with the sight of several generations of Omegas attending. Fathers, sons, and sons' young wives and children, the little girls in purple and gold, and the little boys with some kind of medallions on suggesting that their fathers were Ques, were common. The continuity of the fraternity over generations was very impressive, and my family fit that category.

We had gotten the children settled in their rooms, got them fed, etc., had gone down to the lobby for something and had run across

Bro. Benjamin E. Mays. We talked about my having given him a ride several years ago in Greensboro, North Carolina. It was about 1966 when this happened. He was on his way to Palmer Memorial Institute for some meeting then. He did not have a car but had been perfectly content to walk.

Bro. Mays, then president of Morehouse College, Atlanta, was one of the country's most distinguished educators. He had just then completed his book *BORN TO REBEL*. I wanted the children to see a very well-known black person, to say they knew him. I considered it a part of their education. Brother Mays, always gracious and accommodating, was happy to go up to the room and meet my family. We were up there about 10 or fifteen minutes when the lights in the hotel went out. They stayed out for about 15 or 20 minutes. It developed that some brothers had ordered several servings of pork chops and the trimmings. When the waiter delivered the order someone broke the circuit in the meter room and blacked out the whole hotel. In the darkness the brothers hijacked the load of pork chops, slipped into a prearranged room, ate the pork chops and trimmings, slid the tray into the hall and vacated the building.

Brother Mays and I both discovered that evening what we felt was becoming inevitable, namely that there was a growing gap between the younger more mischievous brothers and the older more settled ones. Neither of us could also get ready for the leather vests which some young brothers were wearing while leaving arms and hairy chests fully exposed. The next Grand Conclave I attended was in Kansas City. This one was much more tame than the one in Houston.

4

Graduate School and Later

The fall of 1960 found my family and me at Washington State University where I began to work seriously toward a Ph.D. degree in sociology. There were only a handful of black students in the university at the time and few opportunities to become involved in activities not directly related to completion of a degree.

The second year two other Ques joined the department to study. David Spurgeon Stamps, now of the University of South Florida and William Julius Wilson, who would later become America's most visible sociologist. We got along very well but the emphasis was on degree-getting. There were only a few blacks on the campus and we needed to pull together insofar as we thought it necessary. But there was such a low degree of overt racism in Washington State that we had to make almost no group demands. I don't recall an incident of segregation while there. If anything, black students were quite wary of bunching too closely together. Maybe there was fear that people would notice us and begin to discriminate. We acted pretty normally and did not have to keep an eye out for discrimination. No issue was made over the fact that three Omegas were in the doctoral program at the same time while there was one Kappa, James E. Conyers, later of Indiana State University, Terre Haute.

As a family we suffered the usual woes of graduate students: not enough money, anxiety over the completion of classes and projects, etc., but I was able to complete all work and dissertation by August of 1963. After that I joined Columbia University's Teachers College as a research assistant and moved to Uganda to carry out this work in educational sociology. We were there two years after which we moved to Lincoln University in Jefferson City, Missouri.

It was at Lincoln that I became reintegrated into the Greek system. There was a thriving graduate chapter at the campus. As at AM&N College, there was some rivalry at the undergraduate level involving the Omegas and other groups, mainly the Kappas and Alphas. All graduate Greeks supported the dances and other activities of other than their own groups. People were very friendly across Greek Lines. Among my friends who were not Omega was the learned Lorenzo Greene, then perhaps the dean of black historians. Greene was happy to report that he, as a young student, carried Carter G. Woodson's books. Greene wrote very well received books on blacks in slavery in Connecticut and Missouri. Dr. Garland Freemen (I believe) an Alpha Man, enjoyed attending the Omega meetings more than he did his own. He was more or less adopted by the graduate chapter and the business of the usual variety was conducted with his being present. I think the only things Freeman did not attend were the initiations.

The Omegas were the most active graduate chapter in the city. It was their yearly formal dance that got most of the attention. They had developed a tradition of serving each other at the monthly meetings. Brothers who had been on the faculty or in the town long enough had acquired nice homes. Lafayette Street, along the campus, was the location of many of the most prestigious homes among the blacks of Jefferson City. The homes had basements which were converted to family rooms, dens, and play rooms which were used as places to entertain. Brothers enjoyed having the chapter over. Wives and girlfriends enjoyed the entertainment as much as the brothers themselves.

Some brothers preferred to entertain the chapter at some hotel or public establishment where the meal could be catered. In 1966, when it was time for me to entertain, though we had just had a new baby, we decided to entertain at Ramada Inn. The meal for about 30 men was about $3.50 each, which did not include highballs. My wife and I did not worry much about the money for we had been saving for it for quite a while. We had bought a home a year before and did not want the group to think we were too strapped for money, though we had four small children. Ownership of a home was very important in the community at Jefferson City. Faculty members who did not own their homes were at very significant social disadvantages.

Not all of the brothers in the city or on the campus took up time with the chapter. Some did not attend meetings or functions. Those who did not were rather deeply involved with other activities, mainly of a scholastic nature. Professor Cecil Blue, one of the promising writers of the Harlem Renaissance, was not very active, though he was always supportive. Neither was Professor Willis Byrd, a noted authority on the study of light spectra. There were just as often persons who were eminent in their fields who were also active in the chapter. And high ranking persons, such as the Dean of the College, Bro. Oscar J. Chapman, really its vice-president, were careful not to become too closely related to Greek Letter activities. They did not want others to think that this was a driving factor in their lives and did not want it to become a focus of claims of favoritism when faculty members and others had to be disciplined.

At Lincoln it soon became evident that some of the most promising faculty members elected not to become Greek. They had not pledged during their undergraduate days. Now they were full-fledged faculty members, or other workers, who realized that Greek life was important in keeping social life going in the community. They attended all functions, particularly if they held degrees and were single. But they would not join. Such persons seemed to have enjoyed perpetual rush.

Although Lincoln University is near the center of the State of Missouri, it was not the center of social activity for black people. St. Louis and Kansas City vied with Jefferson City as centers of black social life. It was more trouble to get to Jefferson City than to either Kansas City or St. Louis. By then, undergraduate chapters were feeling they did not need sponsorship, that they could plan their activities and carry them out, that an adult should not be able to veto their activities. The idea of chaperoning students was also losing ground. In my day, a faculty sponsor had to be consulted on almost all decisions. This gave social rank to the sponsor. It placed the sponsor in position to talk with the most influential persons of the campus for Greek students were important in carrying out most social activities. When students were needed for community work Greek sponsors were called to help with the selections. A number of younger graduate brothers were expected to help with

30   *Sixty Years A Que*

the undergraduate chapter. This did not fall to me perhaps because there were already enthusiastic brothers working with the chapter.

Lincoln was the site of some regional fraternity meetings. The gathering of the men there made things a little more lively. But the regionals did not make it to Jefferson City more than about once each ten years.

(Seated) Kimberly Perry, Aprile Johnson and Marion "Missy" McGee and (standing) Madalyn Anderson and T

5

University of Arkansas

Black Greeks

I have been asked to talk for a few moments about the development of black Greek chapters on the campus of the University of Arkansas. There are many persons here who might paint a picture different from that which I might give. And even I might not have the same attitude toward the meaning of Greek chapters as I had when we tried to get them started in 1974.

We began to think about the need for activities for our young persons as early as 1969 when I joined the faculty of the University. At that time there were many other fronts on which to fight, such fronts as getting more black students on campus, getting black faculty members, agitating for more participation on the athletic teams. Some of you might not know that the very first blacks on the University varsity teams were in 1969. Jon Richardson was the person who suited up then and became a star for the time that he played. He was accompanied by a student who played on the line. His name was Jerry Jennings, now of Ft. Smith.

The late 1960s were a time of activism. Students had causes they wanted to pursue. Their main cause was the rooting out of any vestiges of racism on the campus and in the city at large. Students published their own paper, sat in presidents' offices, challenged racist teachers, exerted themselves in the cause of bringing equity to the campus. Yes, they were flunking out then at about the same rate as they are now flunking out. But that didn't make much difference if one was doing something which was for the betterment of the cause.

By the first few years of the 1970s we could see that students were becoming one-dimensional. Many were doing very good political work, which cost them grade points for sometimes this work took them out of classes. The graduation rate was not high enough to be an encouragement. Some of us wondered what could be done to help black students enjoy the campus more so that they could concentrate on their studies as a natural part of their activities. We had just gotten the BAD Choir going. It is now called the Inspirational Singers. The choir had served as a kind of all-purpose fraternity for blacks. They enjoyed the fraternization and got along very well without a director. There was always some graduate student or well prepared undergraduate who could handle the choir. We argued for and got black students to be on the various cheering squads and into many of the formerly separate activities characteristic of the campus. But one thing remained clear. The Greek societies of the campus were not willing to consider the admission of blacks, though a few did rush during the early 1970s. One fraternity accepted a black student for a pledge but mysteriously the fraternity went defunct shortly before the student was to be initiated. There seemed to be only one choice--to bring black Greeks on the campus. We had to argue with the Panhellenic Council over the matter of houses and campus leadership. We had to alter the grade point requirements for entrance in some cases in order to compensate for what was thought to be the extremely harsh attitude toward blacks getting good grades on campus.

Some blacks did not feel we should bring these societies on campus for they were thought to promote snobbery and ghetto-like behavior. Some of us believed that the healthy competition which Greek life generated on black campuses could be transferred to this university. And we who had read E.F. Frazier's 1959 *Black Bourgeoisie*, or who had lived long enough, knew that black society remained structured around Greek life. In many communities this may be the only social life that may be found. Even today the state-wide Greek dances and other social functions are the main ones in most communities. We thought students should have the opportunity to go Greek. In short, we thought Greek life would be helpful. Indeed, many of the parents of black students were Greek and they wanted their children to follow in their footsteps.

We have not conducted any research to find how Greeks are doing in the real world compared to nonGreeks. The typical University of Arkansas --black Greek chapter is no more than 15 years old. At the 25 year mark we hope to see books written, murals painted, discoveries made, by black Greeks from this institution. We want to see them with fewer broken homes; we want to see them with fewer criminal records; we want to see them standing up and being role models in their communities. That was the hope we had for black Greeks on this campus in 1974 when the first group was chartered here. That remains our hope for them today. We hope that we are not disappointed in maintaining this hope. (Remarks given in the mid-1980s at a gathering of the sisters and friends of the local chapter of Delta Sigma Theta Sorority at the University of Arkansas).

Omega Models

As young man we knew there were people we looked up to. We patterned our lives after them, or what we thought their lives were like. They looked so successful, self-assured, confident, always in command. And they had so much knowledge. Maybe that was what school was supposed to be, to help us find role models whom we could emulate.

The persons we wanted to emulate probably did not know that they were important models for us. It was only years later that I learned that to be so. As we looked up to people before us, as we moved into adulthood, parenthood, professional positions, or exhibited other degrees of achievement or accomplishment, young people began to look up to us. They think about us as we thought about the leaders of the generations ahead of us. Perhaps that is the way nature intends it to be.

But because young people are looking at us, even when we do not know it, and some actually or figuratively patterning after us, it is extremely important not to disappoint them. There is nothing more devastating than to learn that someone whom we had high respect for, looked up to, proved to be less than the sterling characters we had imagined them to be. We hate to have our role models dashed. That is why, possibly, that Ralph Abernathy's revealing some of the last evening indiscretions of Dr. Martin Luther King proved to be so devastating to some. But to others it merely humanized King and showed that he was not much different from all others. And the movie LAST TEMPTATIONS showed that Christ was quite human in his desires and dreams, pretty much like other ordinary men. In looking up to other people we run the risk of having our expectations and visions of their perfection dashed. And some people, many not so noted, go to great extremes to protect their images for they know that what people think of them is not permanent. It is all subject to change.

I thought Professor Tilman C. Cothran, perhaps one of my earliest role models, was the epitome of scholastic and personal excellence. If I could ever lecture like Dr. Cothran much of my life would be complete. Outside the academic sphere, one person who impressed me more than he ever realized was a soldier named Robert Bruce who, though only a Private First Class, was so good in all fields of soldiering that he trained officers. I knew I could never measure up even halfway to Robert Bruce, but if I could bark cadence one-half as well as he could, I would have considered my military career a success.

As I look back from the vantage point of 40 years I find that believing in something and someone for inspiration in my own life was not all wrong. It kept me going, even when it was not extremely clear where I was going or why I wanted to go. And I get a few indications from some of my students and more youthful friends today that some of them think that I may stand as something of a model for them. It is nice to feel that someone else thinks that you are trying to stand for something. A young student was helping me with a paper, gathering and organizing data, etc., while I did the writing. When the paper was about finished I asked her to read it aloud in the office. I had my feet up on the table looking out the window when she began to read. As she did I noticed something very strange. When she finished and asked me to critique her reading, I told her my only complaint was that she sounded so much like me. And she had not recognized that she was. It was then that the two of us realized that she was patterning after me without even knowing it. And not only with respect to how she sounded. The young lady actually believes me to be very intelligent which no logic I can adduce will persuade her otherwise.

I hope that what the student saw in me was the result of how I have tried to live my life which serves as an inspiration to her, and to others, that it was the result of the normal attempts of a person who had taken one of the cardinal principles as a cornerstone of daily life, trying to live it even when the symbols of Greekdom are not evident. It was a long time before the student even knew that I was Greek. My belief is that there are plenty of young people out there, in our neighborhoods, communities, places of work, churches, etc., who look up to us and believe in us and what we stand for. They will have to make their own decisions later in life but while they believe in us let us not disappoint them.

There were other times which I did not know that other people were watching my example. I began teaching high school mathematics in 1956. The principal assigned the sponsorship of the senior class to me. All the activities of the class had to be funneled through and approved by the sponsor. In that class was a rather able athlete named Elijah Pitts, of the little country town where I was born, Mayflower, Arkansas, about 12 miles from Conway. Pitts was an outstanding athlete, all around. He enrolled in Philander Smith College and did well in football. He went on to play professional football with the Greenbay Packers during the glory years of Vince Lombardi. I learned sometime later that Pitts was initiated along the way into the Omega brotherhood. Whether I had a hand in his success is doubtful, but I do remember him as saying he thought highly of me as a teacher. I had moved to Pine Bluff to begin college teaching while Pitts was still at Philander as a student. When I told him of my move he applauded my choice saying that I had a little more talent than they were asking me to show at my old high school. That was a very high compliment.

As I have indicated in earlier pages, the Omegas were quite a popular group so far as the young men were concerned who followed my brother and myself into college. We had looked up to students preceding us in college who had joined the fraternity. It should not have been so unexpected that those who we preceded would see that we had made a good choice and would follow us when they entered college. There was the case of Dr. Joe Norman Manley. He was several years younger than myself. I think he was along with my baby sister. Manley was a good athlete and outstanding scholar from a very good family in the town. He went to some of the best colleges and universities in the U.S. and somewhere along the way achieved a degree in optometry. Manley was initiated into the Omegas, evidently after college. We were not what you would call close friends, nor did we get a chance to fraternize much under the Omega symbols. But from what I knew of him, before his passing at age 39, he was a person trying to make a difference in the community in which he lived. He dared to open his practice in some of the highest rental property in Little Rock at a time when it was thought that a black person had no chance for success. Perhaps the examples the Omegas from Conway set were important in helping men like Bro. Manley decide that he wanted to be a part of what we were trying to represent.

It takes a long time to truly understand the meaning of fraternity. Some of us think that it means attending meetings and making plans for some social function, civic or other activity. In every organization there are people who internalize the organization's outward symbols while ignoring the basic values for which the group stands. Some of the best Omegas, or other Greeks, I know are not very diligent about being parts of chapters. They do more than simply pay their dues. They try to live up to the standards of the group to the very best of their abilities. One brother I had the highest regard for was Dr. Willis E. Byrd, professor of chemistry at Lincoln University in Missouri. Brother Byrd was so busy trying to make certain breakthroughs in the field of spectroscopy that he simply did not have time to attend the meetings and get deeply involved in chapter politics. He never said chapter work was not important but with a small amount of time one has to use it wisely and well. He thought that he could be as much an Omega brother by exhibiting a high level of scholarship as anyone who enjoyed spending time in the social events.

6

Cardinal Principles Examined

The principles on which Omega Psi Phi Fraternity was founded have been adhered to generally by the majority of the men forming the brotherhood. These high standards: manhood, scholarship, perseverance and uplift are ideals which could hardly be challenged by any group. They remain in force from initiation throughout life for most of us, we hope. But the fraternity really knows too little about the extent to which there are deviations from the cardinal principles. Research needs to go into this and various other areas of fraternity.

It is encouraging to read in the *Oracle* and find that so many young men, and some not so young, are still loyal to the abstract principles of the fraternity. There is little gainsaying that upholding these standards makes for overall better citizenship for the principles of Omega are hardly different from the requirements of good citizenship.

The expansion of Omega Psi Phi from an initial chapter at Howard University in 1911 to more than 300 chapters scattered across the country and several foreign countries attest to the belief that brotherhood is a strong force in the social requirements of man. The fraternity is a unitizing force, linking old and young across great cultural chasms such as wealth and poverty; across races. It links collegiate men to their communities for most of the activities and projects involve communities where the majority of the citizens are not college trained. It ties collegians together and offers opportunities for young men to gain a sense of self worth and to stretch for possibilities they otherwise may not consider. And the old line black Greek letter societies had basically the same goals for their participants whether those participants were men or women. The focus has always been on improved citizenship which includes a great swath of possibilities: self-help, group help, achievement, and so on. The fun of fraternization, the dances, activities, and projects of these groups have attracted young people for some eighty years.

But is the fraternity reaching its greatest potential? Are some young people being excluded who need the experience of discipline at a critical time in their development? Are the principles too rigid to allow the participation of more young men and especially those who need the fraternity most desperately?

The principle of scholarship is at issue specifically. Perhaps most young men would be able to meet the ideals of manhood, perseverance, and uplift because they fit most naturally into their everyday activities and socialization. They are the things that one does almost reflexively and if he does not a pledge period of two months could not change him. So the real cutting criterion is the scholarship requirement.

In my undergraduate days our campus required a C average for participation in Greek letter organizations and the local chapters usually required a C+ with some occasionally requiring a B average. We were at all black schools and a student could get evaluated more objectively, so he thought. If he did not get his average, at least he could not claim the instructors and the school were racist. We had not had the wrenching experience of integration and the loss of a sense of identity in the process. We felt we could go to instructors and get help without compromising our values or "eating cheese" to white folks.

The fraternity and black society so badly needed scholars that any youth with talent was encouraged to go as far as he could and so the scholarship requirement encouraged him to hit the books and prepare himself for the opportunity to participate in the uplift of his people. The desire to meet the cardinal principle of scholarship helped many youths to discover their potential.

Many caught fire and went on to enviable careers almost directly as a result of meeting the scholastic requirement for entering and remaining in good standing in the fraternity. In my undergraduate days one could be suspended for not keeping a passing average and the chapter itself could be suspended if it failed overall to maintain a school imposed average.

It would probably be a mistake to change the scholarship principle because the conditions which prohibited black and poor youths from realizing their talent are operative today just as they were 40 years ago when I became an Omega. And yet this barrier prohibits many young collegians from participating. Nearly half of all black students are now found in predominantly white colleges. Many of these colleges are still looking for their first black honor student, their first major in science, their first Phi Beta Kappa. They are still struggling to integrate their staffs with blacks in something other than token numbers. Black youths have few role models and few to turn to because of uncertain rapport with white faculty members who could help them. Some of the best black talent has some of the poorest grades for it is well known that often the most perceptive are the most alienated.

Making a C average at Po Dunk University (practically any white school) with the limitations of alienation and social frustration is about like making a B average at a school where one is well adjusted. Thus, when chapters are opened at majority schools there is difficulty in finding enough people to keep them operative. The revolving door policy of admitting blacks then flunking them out is a reality in many schools which have fairly large numbers of black students. Athletes have very little opportunity to pledge because of a combination of poor grades and little time off for pledging. Because they are on athletic scholarships they are at the mercy of the coach who, if white, may take a dim view of his black stars' engaging in the pledge process.

The process is similar at mainly black colleges. The youth showing up have been badly taught in high schools where the integration process dictated that they teach themselves or go lacking. Black faculty, insisting that the students meet universal criteria of excellence, flunk them out in black schools as rapidly as in white ones. The process is vicious.

Our question is should the youth show he is a scholar by posting an average or better grade to enter the fraternity when it is known he has been handicapped in the learning process? Or should the principle mean he is a potentially promising scholar? If a person is potentially promising we could initiate many more young men who have every opportunity to meet all the cardinal principles of the fraternity.

The Meaning of Uplift

Uplift, or helping of the group farthest down--really assisting black people, has been a main pillar of all black Greek societies. When these societies were formed the principal theoretical influence was that of Booker T. Washington. The emphasis was upon the development of a black society which was so strong and prosperous that all would observe with envy the progress that these former slaves and their descendants had made. Washington literally taught that blacks would have to build their own society and institutions to the extent that they would not be dependent upon any other group. Washington thought that if blacks became outstanding enough in their own communities that the world would beat a path to their door. He measured the esteem in which a group was held by the degree to which they contributed to the economic life of the greater community.

The influence of Washington, though not without criticism by persons such as W.E.B. Du Bois, who thought otherwise, was quite heavy. Washington was accused of advocating separatism of the races, justifying the positions of less than equality which blacks were experiencing, and giving aid and comfort to those who could not envision black people as having legitimate claims to the rights and privileges of all Americans.

When Washington made his Atlanta Cotton States Exposition speech in 1895 Jim Crow had been informally but effectively established in all of the South and de facto in much of the North. America was moving toward two separate societies. The lack of black rights had been taken as a matter of course and there were few legal means for resisting it. The few lawyers and civil rights fighters available could not fight in the South where most of the blacks were centered. Lynchings were still being carried out and the perpetrators never prosecuted. If Washington's speech was considered conciliatory or accommodationist, it must be considered against the backdrop of the reality of life which black people faced. They did not have the means for making the fight they would later wage.

To Washington's credit must be noted his stress on uplift--black people helping themselves--helping each other, erecting businesses, mastering the professions, farming, accumulating property, and doing all those things which would announce to the world that they were capable of economic success. Washington understood that the majority community was unwilling to service the black community. On the foundation of the need for those services black businesses could be built, the community expanded, beautified, and made a sparkling example of what blacks could do once the shackles of slavery were removed.

When the black Greek societies were begun community help became an important feature of their reason for existence, though it was hard for some time for tangible evidence of that help to be identifiable. Blacks were not only receiving little help from any level of government but were actively discouraged from achievement and progress in almost any area of life. There was no secure niche for them, not even in domestic work for women and common labor for men. Any achievement or recognition was gained at very great personal expense. High unemployment rates in both farming and city locations told the story and this was reflected in lives of black families which were very far from the threshold of respectability. Not even the National Association for the Advancement of Colored People had been formed by the time of the organization of the first collegiate Greek letter societies. If there was to be any improvement in the status of black people they would have to accomplish it on their own for they were not the favorite people of the government and the areas in which they lived.

Many blacks had begun to conceptualize the problem in terms of basic differences between themselves and white people. Color provided the separation point. The literature and expressive art of the period before the Harlem Renaissance was basically oriented around the theme of the tragic mulatto. People who became angry because they were not white, because one of their ancestors was white, wrote materials reflecting the concept of marginality which, by the 1930s had become thoroughly established in the literature and theory of sociology. Because of a two-race classificatory system--black and white—all other groups phenotypically in between these had very difficult times locating. They were said to experience trauma because of ambiguous placement. Nowhere were this ambiguity and ambivalence more exemplified than in the writings of marginalized black people. James Weldon Johnson could write a book entitled *AUTOBIOGRAPHY OF AN EX-COLORED MAN*.

Books on blacks passing for white were written quite commonly. There was a certain fascination with the almost white black person, the person who could not fit comfortably into black society where there was no likelihood that he could enter white society. They would not have such a person if they knew he was black.

Phenotype meant much and there was a rush to adopt the white phenotype. If one could get rid of a few black characteristics the better he or she felt. Thus hair was straightened instead of left kinky. Skin lighteners were big sellers in the nickel and dime stores. Even talking proper, meaning talking northern white, became a practice among blacks who were fortunate enough to travel and remain for a while in the North. If one could date or marry a person a little lighter than oneself parents and friends would be happy. If one could find a partner almost white they sometimes were ecstatic. A literal and actual state of war existed between blacks of African phenotype and those with European phenotype or, in everyday language, between dark-skinned and light-skinned blacks.

Marcus Garvey burst on the scene in 1916 fleeing from color conscious Jamaica and preaching "black is beautiful," that black people should abandon America and return to the kingdom of black people--Africa. His movement appealed to a wide spectrum of blacks who thought for the first time in their lives that they were not cursed by being black. They abandoned the "curse of Cain," "Ham, Shem, and damn," argument which had encouraged them to think of themselves as less than other people because they were not white. Very bitter statements linking character to color flew about with abandon, such as, "If you white you all right. If you brown stick around. If you black git back."

Booker T. Washington had been a principal proponent of black self-help. When he died in 1915 the seed had been sewn though there had been opposition from other quarters. Garvey taught that if blacks could not go back to Africa they could work for a separate society in this country. They would have to help themselves to build their own communities. Garvey was jailed for advocating that blacks change their positions in America, though this was done ostensibly for other reasons such as misuse of the mails.

By the time of the formation of Omega Psi Phi Fraternity in 1911 the founders had seen that self-help was the only way out of the black quagmire of poverty and dependency. Every able black male would have to help any other one who needed it. Education and the attainment of skills would not be for private benefit; they would go for group fulfillment. It would be a matter of pulling together for only by pooling of resources would blacks have a reasonable chance of improvement and the reaching of potentials.

Despite the emphasis of Washington and Garvey the idea that lack of whiteness persisted and remained a theme in black writings and art on through the depression and into World War 2. Perhaps one of the last books by a bitter black person, hurt because he was not white, was Richard Wright's BLACK BOY, published about 1946.

Overcoming self-hatred owing to oppression was not easy to achieve, but steps were made in that direction. Following World War II blacks shifted from overconcern with not being white to the achievement of civil rights. They argued and rioted and communicated that one does not need to be white to be either good or to have all the rights which American citizenship purported to assure. A part of the problem of black dependency was that the law was against them. They could wish to be white and work to improve themselves in their own communities to their heart's content but their effects would be less than if they battered down the doors of discrimination. So the focus shifted to the achievement of civil rights.

The excitement of marching, sitting in, laying in, going to jail, and being encouraged by the example of Martin Luther King, Jr., and others, made blacks feel for a moment that there was little else to do after it was possible to get a room in Holiday Inn and to buy a hamburger at McDonald's. The falling of many former segregations: schools, churches, lodges, beaches, water fountains, living places, jobs, political affiliations, etc., led even some black scholars to conclude that major shortcomings by blacks were not, at least by the 1970s, the responsibilities of black people themselves. They were sufficiently integrated into the major society that they could not claim, with credibility, that they were being held back because of race. They could go anywhere and do anything in the society for which they were otherwise qualified. In terms of the black Greeks, what would happen to the requirement that they uplift their people? Did service and help degenerate to mean passing out a few boxes of canned goods at Thanksgiving and Christmas or perhaps a $100 scholarship or so yearly? Or did it mean spending a grand total of 10 hours per chapter year tutoring a single black child from the ghetto?

7

A Tenth Anniversary Talk to Gamma Eta Chapter

Fayetteville, Arkansas, Spring 1984

To the members and guests of Gamma Eta Chapter, Omega Psi Phi Fraternity, and particularly to those who have come from afar to be a part of the festivity of recognizing the 10th anniversary of the founding of this chapter, we humbly welcome you. You are always welcome to Fayetteville and to the University of Arkansas.

Tonight we have an opportunity to reflect for a time on a movement which has swept the majority colleges and universities since the 1960s, that is the founding of Greek letter societies for minority students, mainly blacks, on these campuses. We are all aware of why these societies were begun. In the early 1900s, 1906 in the case of Alpha Phi Alpha, and 1911, in the case of Omega Psi Phi, there were not so many black college students. The full impact of the 1890 Morrill Act, which established land grant colleges in the Southern and Border States primarily for black people was not yet felt. The few students eligible to attend colleges in the North did not feel welcome; their attendance seemed to work a hardship upon the schools and their participation in the usual activities of college life was misinterpreted as meaning they were seeking social recognition beyond the limits which justified their hopes. They would have joined the societies of their colleges had they not been rebuffed. Of course, when there were a few black students on mainly white campuses, a token one or two always found receptivity in majority group organizations. It was when blacks wanted to enroll wholesale in them that their numbers became problematical. It has been the same for many years. The majority schools would take a few especially well-qualified minority students, those who would be easily cooptible into the system. They would be trained as majority people and would largely reject their own group, even their parents who might have been unschooled. The black middle class of professionals who could afford these experiences encouraged them to cast their lot with the more "cultured" group and not with the crude folk known variously as shines, spooks, and spades.

Education has been a precious commodity and the black middle class controlled it after about 1900. They were quite shocked when higher education was placed in the reach of the ordinary youth from the small towns and plantations and youth from these circumstances received opportunities to attain college degrees and compete with the children of the black middle class for positions and respect within within the black community. Thus, long before the founding of Alpha Phi Alpha in 1906, blacks in small numbers had been members of Sigma Chi, Sigma Nu, Kappa Sigma, Chi Omega, and Tri Delta. It was the spirit of racism which swept the country from the end of Reconstruction through 1954 which discouraged the older Greek societies from taking black members and encouraged the setting up of such organizations on white campuses by black members. Usually when black organizations set up parallel to white ones, they take the same names as the white ones. For example, when Richard Allen and Absalom Jones were expelled from the Episcopal Church in Philadelphia, they established the Colored Methodist Episcopal Church. When blacks could not join the Elks, they established the Black Elks. The Moose, Chamber of Commerce, and numerous others were begun. Even Prince Hall Masons grew out of the same condition.

At first the white organizations simply asked blacks to pay a charter fee and then they were initiated by white brothers who never saw them again. Thereafter blacks would perform their own initiations and become black members of organizations which did not accept them as brothers. There might have been black chapters of Sigma Chi, Sigma Alpha Epsilon, or Kappa Sigma, had black people not fully understood that they did not need the names of white organizations to become fully respected. Breaking away from the use of majority names was a step toward breaking away from the dependency hold others had on us; it was a move toward psychological self-determination of our own conditions. No group had a hold on the use of any name or title.

Fraternity was not in the name but was in the quality of brotherhood the members experienced. One did not have to be a Sigma Chi; Omega Psi Phi would be just as good, if not better. In retrospect we did not have to be Colored Methodists. We should have denied Methodism altogether and asserted our own African religions. Frankly, I would have rather had voodoo, as something truly African, than to have been known as a Catholic, Methodist, Baptist, or Presbyterian, something completely alien to me.

But much of what I am talking about is in the past. Perhaps we should not dwell on it too long. The here and now is what is important although we can in no way neglect history. We are, to a very large extent, what history has made us. Nathan Hare, a prominent social scientist, wrote several years ago that we black people are nothing but Black Anglo Saxons; simply white folks in dark skins. Frantz Fanon of the West Indies island of Martinique, wrote that we are black faces in white masks. Abram Kardiner and Lionel Ovesey, two European psychiatrists, have said we have the mark of oppression. All these people, and they are blacks as well as whites, say that we are crazy or that we do not know who we are. William Grier and Price Cobb say that because we do not know who we are--we do not understand the contradictions which history has imposed upon us--we are in a state of rage, thus the title of their book *Black Rage*.

I am ready to reject any notion or conclusion which defines black people as different on any scale of measurement. We are not Omegas because we could not become Sigma Chis. We are Omega because we wanted to be Omegas, because the idea of fraternity as promulgated by Omega Psi Phi appealed to us. It is a matter of interpretation that we automatically would have chosen to be Kappa Sigs or Sigma Chis if we had the opportunity to be. That we have some control over the defining process, that we do not have to accept the interpretations of historians, psychiatrists, sociologists, or anyone else who tries to degrade our humanity by claiming that we are a confused folk because we are not white is a matter of becoming psychologically free.

Today there is a movement on campuses such as ours to integrate the Greek letter societies. In practice this means that blacks will join the mainstream old societies. I think this is a fair movement though I do not see the University making as much of a move to see that white youth join Omega Psi Phi or Alpha Phi Alpha or Kappa Alpha Psi or Phi Beta Sigma, or any of the four old line black sororities. I see it as a move to gut black organizations in the same way that black colleges were gutted and black hospitals and financial institutions were gutted. You may not know that the first step toward destruction of black banks was the opening of white banks to black depositors. The destruction of the black college began with the admission of the first black students to the white institutions. As late as 1969 when I moved to my town I was told that black people were not welcome at a certain bank and so it was about three years before I tried to do any business with them. I guess one could interpret each and every move by the establishment as an attempt to undermine our development. To me this is paranoid thinking. One could argue that each black home bought in a suburb could mean the destruction of black institutions in the inner city since it takes money and talent and incentive out of the inner city. The simple fact is that whenever anyone argues within the confines of race or ethnicity, the problem posed has no solution. Such concepts, to my way of thinking, should be abandoned. They are not helpful to any extent.

If the University presses for the integration of organizations, it should be on the more plausible ground that we may produce a better student, a more wholesome product, a student which will better represent the university and become a more productive citizen. This seems more humane than talking in terms of racial and ethnic proportions.

Not all blacks ought to be Ques or Alphas, Deltas or AKAs. Not all whites need be members of their respective societies. There should be no ethnically identifiable organizations on campus because ethnicity is such a dysfunctional way of structuring any type of social relationship. Several years ago I wrote a piece for our publication, *The Oracle*, in which I discussed the question of our children choosing some other fraternity than that of their parents. We have long had children of the same family who joined different associations but we have probably had fewer children who did not follow in the footsteps of their parents. My father was not a college man so he did not understand Greek life. There was no tradition for me to follow. I followed my brother into the Omegas and he followed a few prominent other natives of my hometown into the Omegas who were ahead of him in college. That is how the tradition was begun in my family. Today, my mother, age 74, would be disappointed if her girls and granddaughters did not marry Omega men, if their choices were college men. She would be upset if her grandsons did not go Omega. She is not a college graduate but she has through the years come to appreciate the Omegas and the type of manhood they represent. Probably every grandparent could say the same about the fraternal choices of their children or grandchildren. Once tradition becomes established it is very hard to break.

I sometimes am quite concerned about the direction that black Greek life has taken. In the early years there was a good deal of snobbery connected with it. On the black campuses you couldn't become an AKA unless your father was a physician or a pastor of a big church. You couldn't be a Kappa unless you played football. You couldn't be an Alpha unless you kept your head in the books all the time. And you couldn't be an Omega unless you were headed for one of the top professions. And on some campuses you had to be a certain color before you could be initiated into certain societies and associations. All of this was stereotype. It never was 100 percent true on any campus, but this was what was in the minds of students and in the minds of much of the public. Today we have the reality of stereotyping. Some of our organizations have become known, at least in stereotype, for their qualities which do not make us look good. For examples, it is said that the Omegas are known to brand people. It is true that some members have gone overboard with brands. Branding is something that requires care and should not be attempted just because one feels like doing it. Those brands may become infected and great damage may occur as a result. Moreover, there may be certain jobs which you cannot hold because you have the distinguishing marks on your arm or chest. In Africa where scarification was common in years past, some tribal members are not eligible for public jobs because they have marks which distinguish them and some are undergoing plastic surgery and skin grafts to get rid of scars which they felt they needed to have to make others know to what tribal groups or associations they belonged. No group forces branding and all discourage it. But it is difficult for a group to control what its members do after they are no longer subject to the restrictions of the group.

Black Greeks have been cited for hazing and a few deaths have been recorded as a result. It is not in the best interest of the fraternity to let our pledging a candidate go beyond common sense and propriety. At Texas A&M a cadet was being hazed by being required to do extra calisthenics. He died and some people are being sued. An Omega initiate became over exuberant after the ceremony and drank a wrong mixture of alcohol and died. We must not let our enthusiasm be so great that we lose our sense of balance. We are in the business of making men, not destroying them. We must also be aware that standards change and that the mark of a good Greek is not how much punishment he or she can take. There is never any need to humiliate or punish any initiate in the process of his becoming one of our members.

I notice a lamentable decline in the averages of Black Greeks on campus. According to some sources some organizations have no one who is not on probation. People have been initiated who do not have acceptable grade point averages. The Omegas require a 2.5. Some argue this average is too high, that on a racist campus a 2.5 on a 4 point scale is about as hard to reach as a 3.5 on an all-black campus for on the latter campus one does not have to deal with the factor of racism.

Frankly, I do not believe a 2.5 is too high if students understand what their real business on the campus is. They should know that the reason for coming to the University is not to pledge a Greek society. Their real business is to get a good education, which includes a good social education to complement the academic one. It is good to be Greek but the society you choose does not want you and will not extend full brotherhood or sisterhood to you if you are a drag on the GPA or if you are short in meeting some of the other principles for which the group stands. They want you to help the group and you cannot help them by being on probation, being in jail, being unemployed, if you could hold a job, being dirty when you could be clean, when you have no goals when all are expecting you to not merely have goals but to serve as an inspiration to others who would like to adopt you as a model. The image of Black Greeks as party people needs to be altered. Yes, we like parties but they are not to conflict with the cardinal principles of manhood, scholarship, perseverance, and uplift.

There are a few other fads which I notice in Greek life today which we did not have during my time. We sang, carried lanterns, dressed in turbans, polished big brothers' shoes, wrote poetry, memorized poems and ran errands. But mostly we tried to keep up our grade point averages for we wanted it known that we were trying to meet some of the standards of the fraternity.

One fad I do not understand is "stepping." I have tried to discover where the idea of stepping or its practice originated. I had not seen it until I came to Fayetteville, Arkansas in 1969. They did not do it at Lincoln University in Missouri. And we did not do it at my undergraduate school in the late 1940s and early 1950s.

I racked my brain for some years and the solution came to me just a few days ago. "Stepping" is a variation of the Stockade Shuffle which is, or certainly was, done during the Korean War, and probably during the last part of World War II. There have always been a disproportionate number of blacks in the Army or military stockades. In the stockade or brig, in the case of the Navy, a part of the program is to maintain physical fitness and military bearing. But there is not much else to do. Black soldiers, in order to pass time, frequently organized into small groups, perhaps five or six men, elected a drill sergeant and did dismounted drill. Whatever they did was contrary to the way drilling was to be conducted, according to the manual. They modified the manual and marched in unapproved ways. The commanders tried everything they knew to keep blacks from doing the stockade shuffle and soon it became a way of spending time on regular posts. It was a black way of innovating and at the same time showing what they really felt about the correct way to drill. Black soldiers worked harder on the stockade shuffle than they did on approved dismounted drill. To be honest their drills made the approved dismounted drills look very dull. So I understand that stepping is a way of expressing a group's individuality. I don't think the adding of the vulgarities to it makes it any more colorful or expressive.

The stockade shuffle was the black soldier's own invention. Like so much else that blacks invented, it was created out of the conditions in which he found himself. He had tried to live by the manual, but the rules placed great restrictions on his performance. When the military services were integrated it was not merely a matter of assigning blacks to white units, or vice versa. Black soldiers, in particular, brought to the units ways of looking at life, and attitudes toward soldiering which were foreign to those who had not lived such as they had, or under similar restrictions. Throughout life the black man has had to adjust to conditions not to his liking, indeed to those which were actually against him. He had to make do with what he had, in the situation in which he found himself. Although black soldiers were outstanding in the various branches of service, the enlisted men, in particular, even though they might have become career soldiers because of the security it provided, were never thoroughly enamored of military life. Their first choice was outside life. There would probably never be a Sgt. Carter among them because they were not so likely to take soldiering seriously. For them it was simply an eight to five job, even if one had to be on duty 24 hours a day. Their hearts were not into it and they did not become emotionally attached to it.

Their tendencies to make light of military life, while carrying out orders, became distinguishing characteristics of black soldiers. A noncom would give every reason why men under his command would not want to do an exercise, or execute an order, but then he would insist that it be carried out to perfection, not because he believed in it, but because he thought people ought to do the best when assigned a duty. The black noncom tried to insist that there be a break between what men were expected to do while on duty and what they might do when off duty. If they wanted to play military games when off duty, he would not be too critical.

Partly because black soldiers were often of lower rank, therefore drawing less pay, and because they had been taught to be verbally contemptuous of military service, it was easier for them to engage in such antics as the stockade shuffle. They did not have money to leave the post, to go to town, or on leave. Many sent their allotments home to relatives who depended upon them for support. The small amounts of money enlisted men had after their allotments were sent home could be lost in crap and card games and the rest of the month could be spent without funds. If no one lent them money they would adjust to the lack of it by engaging in those activities which did not cost money.

The stockade shuffle was a way of killing time while allowing the men to engage in very close order drill which was contrary to the way drilling was written in the manual. For instance, if the manual called for a normal march step of 30 inches, with arms swinging 6 inches to the front and 3 inches to the rear, black soldiers might shorten the step to 10 inches and swing arms in such as way as to violate the regulations. If one foot is to be placed before and parallel to the other in regular march, black soldiers might keep the same foot always before the other while dragging the other behind. The effect was a parodying of the rules of march. There were standard commands for drill which most soldiers know. Blacks made up new commands and all sorts of innovations were made, all of which were illegal.

The stockade shuffle allowed men to play at command when their real positions would not permit it. A good drill man might be a private but would be recognized as an expert cadence caller by his stockade shuffle buddies. He might call cadence and orders better than anyone, with better rhythm and clarity of voice.

Shuffle buddies were usually a fairly closely knit group, though they need not have been to the stockade. They spent much time fraternizing together probably because they were less bound by the rules of rank. Stockade and shuffle buddies were generally privates.

The stockade shuffle is a style of march assumed to have originated by soldiers who were in the stockade as a way of killing time when they had no other duties to perform. It is a highly improvised and colorful set of steps with its own unwritten but well understood, by them, methods of execution. It is performed mainly by the lowest ranking enlisted men and to engage in it may be a violation of orders from commanders. A minimum of two persons are required to do the shuffle, one man to give the commands and another to carry them out. However, a squad of 9 men or more may occasionally be seen surreptitiously doing the stockade shuffle.

8

Beyond Civil Rights

I thought about the competition which existed among the Greeks on my campus when I was a young man. 1 believe it was healthy in concept because it encouraged groups to exert themselves in the helping of others, especially when that help was toward meeting the main values of the groups. It was exciting to see the competition carried out at regional and national levels. When the competition was completed the groups came together to support one another in the putting over of dances and other social functions. Each Greek association at the national level adopted some project which gave it some visibility and national thrust. Nearly all of them supported certain longstanding civil rights groups such as the NAACP and the Urban League. During the King Movement they all supported the Southern Christian Leadership Council, with cash and as individuals. Sometimes members of Greek societies were jailed in sit-ins, or suffered other personal indignities. They may have helped individuals who were not members of their associations. I believe, though, that Paula Giddings speaks for more than the members of Delta Sigma Theta Sorority when she states that the idea of the sorority was not to transform society but to transform individuals The same seems to have been the case of the fraternities.

There was always a kind of reluctance of the Greeks to become associated with civil rights work, a principal task confronting all blacks before in passing of the Civil Rights Act of 1964. Of course, part of that reluctance lay in the fact that the blacks of the professional classes worked at public jobs, teaching, post office, hospitals, military, etc., and were vulnerable to severe censure should they become involved in other than nonpolitical activity. Independently employed persons such as ministers, lawyers, and private practice doctors could withstand the economic reprisals almost sure to come from majority group members opposed to black mobility. However, if a Greek brother did assert himself in this work and experienced some success, his notoriety was duly accepted and he was hailed as a hero by the group. By associating the Greek society with the famous person it could be implied that it was the society which was pushing the achievement. In time the groups could put up long lists of achieving individuals in this area of achievement or that. These individuals became the focus of many nighttime discussions among young Greeks asserting that their group or members were more or less outstanding than another group or its members.

From 1955 to the end of the protest period Greeks on campuses were seldom the leaders. They had been trained to work more in the tactics of non-confrontation. They were more scholarly and had greater confidence in the effectiveness of negotiation and preparation as means of opening up the system. They had come often from homes with middle class aspirations, if not achievement. They did not want their names in the papers for having been jailed even for civil right work for they felt these records would accompany them through life and be used against them to prohibit their mobility. Thus, the four young men who sat in at Woolworth's to desegregate the lunch counter were not Greek. The Greeks and independents had the same goals but not the same means for reaching them. There were opportunities to compete against the other groups at a much more local level. As I became older I joined other organizations opened up to blacks about 1980. Much of the program of organizations which opened up, such as the Rotary, Chamber of Commerce, Lions, Kiwanis, Exchange, etc., paralleled that of the adult black Greek societies. But there was still a soft spot in my heart for the Omegas. There always had been, and would remain. But civil rights work took a different focus. There was still much to be done in the black community. We could fight drugs and crime, conduct literacy drives, serve as role models for youth and in many other ways bring our talent and enthusiasm to bear on the community. We would not be prohibited from working with the black community even though we worked in the larger community. There were many areas in which Omega men could get involved. When I was a young man I was a scoutmaster. This was very hard work laid on after my regular job as a high school teacher. I did it, not so much because I wanted to advance the name of the fraternity. Service had by then become something I thought was a part of the expectation of community-minded people. Service is what had helped us rise up out of the doldrums of discrimination. We had to work to make our community shine.

We were not welcome in the white community. And there was always a great deal of church and lodge work to be done. Maybe some of this work was due to the fact that I was connected with the school and the community had thought that teachers knew how to do practically anything. We were supposed to have more knowledge than anyone else as well as the time to render service. So even if we had not been members of organizations such as Greek letter societies we would be expected to do community service while remaining on the teaching payroll. It all looked thankless but when the students under our supervision began to become a little outstanding they often nodded in our direction as giving them inspiration and that often was enough to keep us active. Today it is more difficult to get blacks to undertake service. They have often moved out of the black community and are increasingly unfamiliar with its needs. They work in jobs in the majority community and are unwilling to take on extra duty, even when it is service. The black middle class have been noted by such scholars as William Wilson, also an Omega brother, as having vacated the black inner city community, taking their expertise and energy with them, leaving the black ghetto without role models. These communities then fall prey to drugs, vice, and disorganization.

Of course, in the days of segregation the black community was the only source of recognition for other blacks. They gained their status from work with the community and many were glad to work therein for they craved a little recognition. Those positions as head of this lodge, this Sunday School, that small business, this or that activity were very important to people who had practically no way of gaining status and recognition. Perhaps the *Chicago Defender*, the *Pittsburgh Courier*, or the *Kansas City Call* would pick up a story about them and they would become well known. There was never any problem with the preachers of the biggest churches or the presidents of the biggest or most prestigious black colleges. They always had somewhere to speak and someone would find their pictures in papers and their wives or girl fiends would be featured in black society. In time John Johnson could found *Ebony* on the basis of gossip about life among the black bourgeoisie. We were so hungry for recognition. And occasionally someone quite humble in terms of community service would get recognized for trying to help the community progress.

But mostly the community suffered for want black leadership then, just as it does today.

The black community was then not so disorganized as the ghetto is today. Though the houses were poor, people had poor jobs, families were large, many children existed while the whereabouts of their fathers remain mysterious, it was not dangerous to walk down the street or leave one's door unlocked. People knew each other and respected them, to some extent. There were occasional shootings and stabbings but these had not reached the epidemic proportions of today.

E.F. Frazier, the sociologist, had chided the black middle class for keeping its mind on status symbols, the substance of success clearly escaping them. He was particularly harsh on the Greek letter societies. He thought some persons were so enamored of this life that they literally lived from one ball or cotillion to the next. For them Greek society was the epitome of social climbing. This life filled all their status needs. They spent lavishly to buy the tuxedos, gowns, drinks, limousines, foods for aftersets and other symbols to announce their participation in society. And their associates were often other Greeks who shared their own attitudes and behaviors.

The small cities in which most of the chapters are found do not have enough Greeks to spend that much effort on social functions. One has to travel some distance, at some expense, to be active in these activities. Some cities are able to capitalize on the needs of the Greeks for such purposes. For instance, parents want their girls to be presented as debutantes. But in the small cities there is no way for them to be presented. In Little Rock, for instance, as many as 40% of the girls presented in the Alpha Phi Alpha Debutante Ball over the past ten years have been out of town or out of state. The Omega Statewide Dance held in Hot Springs during the past 10 years or so has a large number of its several hundred participants coming from out of town or out of state. The Kappa Boat Ride in Washington, D.C., seems to have had the same kind of response. Years ago in Arkansas one had to go to Pine Bluff or Little Rock to participate in adult Greek social functions. The towns where most of us worked were simply too small and the number of Greeks of any single group too few to justify chapters. So most of us threw ourselves into service activities on an individual basis because we thought service remained a part of our general orientation. Being Greek helped that orientation.

With the politics of civil rights diminishing in importance, and other groups taking up functions which Greek groups engaged in earlier, what is there left for black Greeks to do other than socialize? I have long thought that there are many things to do. The challenge is of a different order. We may still be about the business of helping young people reach their fullest potential. For example, years ago the Deltas sponsored a Jabberwock. Really this was a contest of short plays. Groups had to pay a small fee to enter the contest. Then they had to write and direct their own plays. The best were presented at a convocation or Saturday evening activity. The campus looked forward to the week of the Jabberwock.

The Jabberwock was outstanding training for aspiring playwrights. It was a good way to have students practice their organizational skills. Getting a group to learn parts, practice, develop stage sets, etc., was very integrated training. Whether they won or lost was not important. Jabberwock helped uncover imagination and talent. Although Jabberwock was a Delta project, all Greek chapters in the state, then limited to those on campuses at Arkansas AM&N College and Philander Smith College, generally participated. The State Jabberwock was held at one or the other campuses and showcased the winning plays.

I would like to see a video Jabberwock. Chapters would do their own video skits according to specifications. The principles of organization, working together, filming, etc., would be accomplished as in the old Jabberwock. These could be shown during Martin Luther King Month. There could be statewide or regional competitions. The main goal would be toward uncovering talent among young people to get them involved in something constructive, to teach them something. In this way Spike Lee could get a little competition.

One of the important values of all Greeks is scholarship. I feel that the young brothers do not understand the importance of this value, at least not to the extent that they want to make learning a lifelong thing. Not enough black Greeks are writing novels, composing plays, completing art, writing music, etc., and showing that they are becoming scholars or people of the mind. The love of learning to the extent that one does it as a matter of course is what I have in mind when I talk about scholarship. Brothers like the late Early Thorpe, a very respectable historian, Carter G. Woodson, the historian, Langston Hughes, the novelist, and Benjamin E. Mays were not merely men trying to qualify for prestigious academic honor societies. They loved learning and by so loving became upholders of the prime value of scholarship. For them scholarship was more than the amassing of a high grade point average. It meant they were attempting to make a contribution to the fund of knowledge.

9

The Meaning of the Pledge Period

If I were a Dean of Pledgees today what would I tell my pledges? I would probably expect them to know the material that has been assigned in a handbook, such material as chapter and national history of the fraternity. I would expect them to know the philosophical foundation on which the organization stands: what the founders hoped would be accomplished by having the candidates go through a period which we call pledging. I would expect each candidate to show evidence of trying to stand for some of those ideals in his own life and to show signs of internalizing these ideals so that they would be meaningful throughout life.

Now what does the pledge period teach? It is designed to teach a number of things. One of these is discipline. Experience shows that this period of a few weeks is the most discipline that some of us have ever received in our lives. It looks hard to get up at 5:00 a.m. and go to a Big Brother's room to wake that person up, only to learn that the person is not at home or is already up and perking. One may be detailed to polish someone's shoes when they don't need polishing. Once you show that you can follow orders, many of which you disagree with, you will find that you have mastered one step on a long ladder which you will face in life. No matter where we stand or sit in life there will always be people who are in position to tell us what to do. Discipline also teaches self control.

But as you learn to take orders, you also learn to give them for pledging teaches leadership as well as fellowship. You should learn how to guide others. This is why you will be expected to take command of your pledge group from time to time, to show that you can perform in a leadership capacity. How this will be done will vary from group to group, but in every pledge group, you will be expected to learn to move forward as a leader, to have people depend upon you for your leadership. This will also help your self confidence for you will learn that people value your thought and your ideas.

Pledging teaches respect for others, which basically is unselfishness. We live on a small planet, in a small community, in a small family. We must learn to get along with others without hostility. Your pledge group will be made up of people of different backgrounds. This is important. Some you think you do not like and never will like. Some won't like you. You will claw and scratch at each other, but you must operate like a family--together. This is why sometimes you are asked to dress in uniform, to do something together, if nothing more than washing cars on a cold day to earn money for some project. Respect for others comes from knowing others and working with them through thick and thin.

As you develop respect for others above and below you in their stations in life, you develop a deeper respect for yourself, a new attitude toward yourself. If you can get along with all these people and these big brothers, satisfying them all in their reasonable demands, you will have your own self-concept improved. You can't be so bad.

Pledging will bring out those who need to be brought out and quiet those who need to be quieted. All should be improved in the process.

Whatever organization you choose has service as one of its mottoes. Pledging helps you to better understand that you must be a servant, in accordance with the biblical quotation, "Let him who would be chief among you also be your servant." This does not mean becoming a servant. It really means helping those who need it, and doing so willingly. It is not noblesse oblige. It is something you believe in. When these organizations (black Greeks) were begun we had few qualified people who could help us. In the first 20 years or so of the 20th century, most of the eight organizations which today make up the old black Greek letter system, our people needed all the help we could get. We could not afford to have our best minds, those who had been fortunate enough to get any degree of college, separated from those of us who needed help the most.

In time partying became mixed with service. Today the two are carried on together. Money is raised for scholarships, worthy causes, talent building, etc., but there is also time for partying at the gala balls--national, state, and local. But the emphasis is on service.

Each organization stresses scholarship. As 17 to 21 year olds, you are not going to put as much emphasis on scholarship as you might. And may I emphasize that the current grade point is not an important predictor of what you may achieve as a scholar. A scholar loves leaning and seeks it constantly. He or she tries to add to what is known. Each organization has many men and women who have dedicated themselves to scholarship, not just accumulating honor roll grades in college, but seeking knowledge through research and sharing what they have found out through the writing of books, articles, and materials which indicate that they are people who use their minds. Some of our best known scholars were Greek. So when your group tries to get you to bring up your average it is to help you develop your mind, to reach for the unknown, to make something happen through your knowledge.

I hope that pledging will not teach you snobbishness. And I hope it will help you get rid of it if you are snobbish. Wearing the shirt and the letters of a Greek organization will not make you more, but it will give people a different attitude toward you. They will expect more of you because they know you have had a different experience. And it is important to remember that one Greek is as good as another, and that one person is as good as another. Yet you stand for the best that social experiences can make you. So do not let your Greek letters go to your head. They will not pay your bills. If you fail to live up to the standards of your organization you will disgrace yourself only.

Be friendly to other Greeks, as well as to other people in general. In some situations one group does not support the activities of others, or certain people are automatically excluded because he or she is not of the right Greek society. Pledging should make you more appreciative of other groups. And it is my hope that the pledge period will permit you to know something about the other societies as well as your own so that you will know that though wearing different colors and symbols, Greeks are one big family where members have different names. They are all trying to do the same things--to make better people out of you.

In pledging don't be a cry baby. Don't be a quitter. Take your medicine as long as it is reasonable. And there are procedures for turning in people who ask you to do unreasonable things. You are not required to do anything unreasonable, such as giving big brothers or sisters money, or allowing the use of your car. In a meeting such as this it is hard to resist repeating what I did as a pledge 57 years ago. We tried to beat the system. We hid out in other peoples' rooms, left town to attend funerals of grandparents who had passed several times, refused to answer the door when big brothers called, studied under blankets with flashlights so they would not see a light in the room. We did all those things and today when I see the brothers and pledgees we have the best old times. We don't remember who we didn't like and whose nose we could bloody as soon as we got off the line. And we sweated and worried about getting blackballed. Those were normal worries. But I believe your leaders are fair and will evaluate you fairly. It is impossible to reduce anxiety totally in any unknown situation.

For many of you this will be a status change. Some of you will have to come down from being somebody on campus to being nobody. But you can do it. Remember, quite often a foundation has to be torn down for a much stronger building to be built.

I have made many friends by being Greek and I don't believe I ever lost a one as a result of being Greek. Differences don't seem so insurmountable when you have something in common, such as being Greek. I believe going Greek is a good experience for the majority of people who decide to pledge and that, overall, those who decide not to pledge, will be the poorer in the long run. Pledge while you are young, when your mind is ready for that experience, when your body is ready, when you don't have the responsibilities of full adulthood. I know some can't do it at the time they wish, but whenever they do, I believe they will be better off. I am happy I went Greek and I believe you are doing the right thing by doing so. I wish you luck during your pledge period and look forward to seeing you in a few weeks in your respective shirts proudly displaying your symbols.

10

From Fun to Service

When black Greek societies were formed they were modeled on the order of white societies which had denied blacks entry because of discrimination. The white societies had been aimed at promoting literary work at first, particularly Phi Beta Kappa, begun in the 1700s at William and Mary College. They then became associated with fun-making and fraternity members in particular were soon known for special types of behavior. The sororities were generally much more subdued and stressed the qualities of femininity and ladyhood to a greater extent than the males attempting to stress manhood. Some of the fraternities were like the old drinking clubs of the European universities which did not become formally organized and chartered. They engaged in a wide variety of behavior which sometimes was beyond the usual pranks and antics of college students. They engaged in club sports and challenged other students or out-of-school groups in a variety of activities.

But there was not as much a category of behavior called collegiate in Europe as there was in America. European students were usually somewhat older than American students studying for the same degree. They were more heavily screened than American students and therefore were more homogeneous. There were more American colleges and a wider variety of students representing many backgrounds were enrolled.

By the time that blacks had become interested enough to feel that they were missing something by not having Greek societies on their campuses, the pattern of Greek life had been set. Greeks were relatively exclusive groups limiting their membership to those of their choices. In order to become members candidates had to subscribe to the practices dictated by those already members. Adults tried to control the practice but hazing became associated with Greek life wherever it was found. The blackball, or negative vote, was used to control those who wanted to be admitted. To evade the blackball the students generally had to endure considerable hardship and degradation, often of a public nature. Because all students entering had to engage in this type of activity, though it was not uniform from group to group, or even from chapter to chapter, or from time to time on the same campus, it was not generally thought of as discriminatory. Some individuals made fairly widely recognized reputations for excessively pledging members and they became the scourge of some groups. It would not be unfair to say that they discouraged many members who otherwise would have joined the organizations.

Although there was a heavy emphasis on scholarship in the black societies, particularly for entrance, keeping up the scholastic emphasis after admission was more easily said than done for some. The stress of the organization was fun, though it was mixed sometimes with a small degree of community service. The major service function of almost any of the societies was the gift of a scholarship to some individual already on campus or to some younger person planning to enroll in college. After the scholarship it was the dances, parties, and sets which the members looked forward to. Wearing the Greek symbols was quite important for many members of the associations for they provided them with identities and recognition they would have hard times acquiring if they were not Greek society members. And because these activities cost money, fundraising was always an important part of the agenda of the black Greek society.

The leaders of the black societies understood that there needed to be a change in activities of the Greeks. During the civil rights movement of the 1960s these societies continued basically to pattern after the older white societies and concentrating on fun, dances and harassment of new members. There were a few progressive chapters here and there which kept their eyes on the basic principles for which their groups stood. The undergraduate students, having been taught that there was a certain amount of degradation that new candidates should go through in order to be admitted, continued

From Fun to Service   67

to engage pledges in secret activities in violation of the operating procedures of those organizations. It was difficult to get them to change. They say they were "boarded" and insisted on having the opportunity to "board" others. Pledge meetings were often referred to as "board meetings" where students were paddled. But, during the years that I have been a member, having seen many probations, I must say that I never saw a candidate paddled except when he was heavily padded. We had to wear pillows and books. When the brother hit the pledge who had taken up a three point stance, there was a frightening noise, but board did not touch flesh. The force might have been enough to push a pledge forward, but there was almost always more noise than there was hurt.

There was one practice called wiping smiles off faces which could have been dangerous. It involved placing a hand over he candidate's face, fingers at the temples, then dragging it down sharply causing lips to pop. If students had problems involving the face, unusual dental work, etc., this was not practiced.

The most serious members of the societies generally had something more important to do than harass candidates for admission. But for some members this was the highlight of their membership. They lived for the opportunity to belittle pledges and some are known to have driven many miles, or missed work or study time for this purpose. In a few cases pledges were hurt in the process or killed. Generally this happens when students become more enthusiastic about pledging candidates than the rules allow. When they go outside the rules they are more likely to engage in behavior over which they might later be sorry.

It was hard to change the groups from fun and hazing to service. And just what would constitute service in the black community? Many civil rights had already been won by the 1970s and emphasis on work in the community was deemphasized in favor of showing that there were the leisure and freedom to excuse one from preoccupation with the improvements of the black community. Some members have alleged that they wanted to join the Greek societies for fun, not to spend most of their time in service projects. They thought there were enough of these service organizations already.

But the national officers kept the idea of service before their groups and soon were able to get their focuses changed so that they could be recognized as service groups for income tax purposes, which is to say they were non-profit organizations. There were a few national projects which all black Greek headquarters agreed upon, such as support of the United Negro College Fund. Others adopted Africa projects as well as local ones, mostly dealing with the granting of scholarships. It has been very hard to get the groups to be extremely serious about their service projects for they have not made the change to the idea that the groups are now service groups rather than purely for fun.

11

Favorites

I have wondered what it would be like to try to list the Omegas who could be set up as models for young men and women of any ethnicity or culture. I am not sure that notoriety is the best criterion to be used to determine such a listing. Perhaps any such listing would be quite subjective. But since it is a personal list, unofficial, perhaps the choices I make would be my own and not subject to a great deal of debate.

There are many persons who meet most of the criteria which the fraternity notes as its cardinal principles. Maybe brothers would like to read what we wrote in *The Oracle* some years ago discussing the most famous Omegas. That article is included in this set of readings for I think it sets the stage for the discussion about to be rendered herewith. Perhaps there are brothers who best exemplify each of the cardinal principles and perhaps each brother would like to make up his private list.

It is not the intention herewith to try to place the Cardinal Principles in order for one is just as important as the other and all four are required to complete the personality of any brother. Each principal is in fact a composite rather than a unitized factor. Each is an ideal type and as such is difficult to break down into the smallest components. Nobody knows exactly what goes into Uplift, Scholarship, Manhood, or Perseverance. These are values which have no real boundaries. But there are brothers I think are good representatives of each of them.

Manhood

I look for a person who is able to take a great deal of pain without flinching. This does not mean that we are talking about a superman, not even an athlete, but someone who is strong in the way that good men have always been strong and able to rise to the task when the chips are down. The brother who tries to keep his family together when there are temptations to abandon it because of the difficulties of holding a job or against the obstacles which beset so many black people. To me manhood is one of the most important of the Cardinal Principles, as each is important for, as noted already, they must be taken as a package. A real man may not have all the advantages but does not let the disadvantages get him down. Because of the deceptive suggestion of manhood, it looks like it is a value very easy to reach for all Omegas are thought to be men. I do not have in mind the chest-beating, the posturing, the branding which is proscribed or not encouraged by the fraternity, or the brusque way that some young brothers think they must behave with women in order to exhibit manhood. I think manhood means responsibility and the making of every effort to meet legitimate responsibilities.

As I have worked in various environments and visited many brothers, though I have not made a study of them all, one brother seemed to stand out in my mind as a representative of manhood, which does not mean he did not meet the other Cardinal Principles. This brother is Robert McDaniel of New York City. Brother McDaniel was a mathematics major in college. He was a pretty good one, we were told. He seemed always to know what to do. He never got down, one never knew when things were going against him. And he has shown that same quality throughout his adult life.

There are many brothers who have exhibited the quality of manhood to a very great extent. No one stands out more than Bayard Rustin who spent 28 months in prison for conscientiously objecting to military service during World War II. Rustin stood up for what he felt was his duty with the consequences diminishing in significance.

Scholarship

By scholarship I mean a love of learning to the extent that one goes far beyond the call of duty in finding out that which he and others do not know. Scholarship has been a cornerstone principle. Exhibition of early scholastic tendencies tells us much about the future behavior of the brother, or at least some think it does. The scholastic requirement is biased toward persons who might later show much progress in that field. A famous coach once said, "If a dog is going to bite he will bite as a pup." Similarly, if a man is going to be scholarly he will show some signs of it during his early life. Omega needs scholars, not just to advance the fraternity, but because scholars contribute so much to the development of the community. They are the thoughtful people, the idea people, and the philosophers. Sometimes their scholarship makes a difference in the way people look at themselves or at the world. Although there are many Omegas of outstanding achievement in the field of scholarship, the one who stands out in my mind as perhaps the best representative of it is Carter G. Woodson. His persistence in learning about the life and history of black people which finally led to the development of Negro History Week and to Black Culture Month, and his zeal in trying to help black people know more about themselves are well known.

Perseverance

Very closely related to both manhood and scholarship is the value of perseverance. Some brothers simply will not quit even when faced with enormous obstacles. We saw candidates who wanted to join the fraternity but who, because of poor scholastic preparation owing to attendance at segregated schools, persisted years in the reaching of their goal. The ability to "hang in" is a very important quality. It is very significant in keeping one's eye on the prize. Jesse Jackson is a good example of perseverance. He sees a goal and is not deterred from reaching it though there are many obstacles to be overcome. Brother Douglas Wilder, now the first black to become an elected governor, must have persisted beyond the requirements of ordinary expectation.

But there are cases which are at least as impressive as these noted which illustrate the quality of perseverance. In the days when black people were not encouraged to acquire higher degrees there were those who persisted when others folded their tents and decided that their efforts would not be rewarded. It looked like the whole experience was one in seeing how much one could take, particularly in the attainment of advanced degrees. And there were almost no channels of redress when the reasons for their failure were not because of their own ineptitude.

Ossie Davis and Ruby Dee were very well known when I was in graduate school in 1960 at Washington State University. William Davis, Ossie's brother was studying to earn a doctoral degree in nutrition. Everywhere he turned there was an obstacle. He seemed unable to get all of his ducks lined up in a row. This or that professor could not be satisfied. Brother Davis became more determined the more he was thwarted in the reaching of his goals. He played a very respectable organ and was in some demand at the local churches. But his goal as a nutritionist dogged him.

I do not know how long Brother William Davis had been at Washington State University before I arrived, but I left in 1963 before he did. I lost track of him but heard that he landed in Texas and was working in his chosen field. We all experience hardship and trials in movement toward our goals, but those who will not quit are the ones whom we all must respect. Brother William Davis gets my vote for being among the most persistent and persevering brothers I have ever encountered.

Uplift

Who has done most to help people? It is unarguable that black people have required that many of their people work in their behalf and there is no shortage of candidates for this recognition. Whatever a person is doing which is legal and moral could be considered as helping black people. The pastor who devotes his life to working in a small parish, practically without recognition, in order that the community may find the encouragement to pull itself up, or at least not to fall further behind, is really uplifting the race. The teacher who toils in the classroom without adequate recognition or remuneration, the lawyer who files cases in behalf of black people without any chance of receiving just compensation are both uplifting the people. Even the small businessman who opens a store in the ghetto or black community to render a service and to provide a role model for the people in another vein, is uplifting. There are professional up-lifters--those connected with organizations which have funds and influence to attack segregation and discrimination--who should not be overlooked. And there is the medical doctor who uses his skill with only a chance of being paid in kind. How far would black people get without persons with this kind of dedication to the mobility of the people.

Uplift was formerly thought of as charity work, no matter by whom it was done. Each black person was believed to have a duty to help those below, even at some sacrifice in income or even notoriety to oneself. After the death of Martin Luther King, Jr., there was something of a turning away from the practice of uplift by individuals who were willing to do work toward the betterment of the race as a matter personal choice.

My two candidates for highest recognition for uplift are Charles Drew, the blood plasma specialist, who used his knowledge of the chemistry of blood to perfect techniques for saving blood which would save thousands of lives throughout the world. His work was uplift on a scale grander than most of us can visualize. Ironically, when he was injured in a car wreck he was not able to profit, according to some accounts, from the knowledge about blood he helped perfect. He could not get a blood transfusion at a segregated hospital.

Robert Gill has provided a glimpse of the next candidate I think would receive highest recognition for his community service and uplift of his people. He was Homer G. Phillips who was connected with nearly every movement to advance the cause of black people. The 607 bed Class A, Homer G. Phillips Hospital, affiliated with the Washington University School of Medicine, is a permanent memorial to Phillips. This Howard University Law School graduate, 1903, was murdered in 1933 by gangsters in a legal dispute.

Hopefully each generation of Omegas will be able to commemorate the men who made very great impressions on them as they tried in their special ways and fields to live up to the Cardinal Principles and thereby advance the cause of the citizenship of mankind and that of the Fraternity.

12

Talking to the Deltas

One of the nicest things that has happened to me during my 40 years of Greekdom happened recently at the Delta Sigma Theta house at the campus of the University of Arkansas, April 28, 1990, The occasion was the reunion of the black alumni of the institution, which goes back to 1948 when the University, then 77 years old, began to readmission of black students. There had been none for about 75 years. A few hundred alumni and persons who had attended the university at some earlier time gathered for a weekend of festivities. The Greek societies made their entry on the campus in 1974, when the first line of Omegas were initiated.

Aside from the historic connection of the Deltas and Omegas, which dates back from the founding of the two organizations, the Omegas in 1911 and the Deltas in 1914, the young ladies of that sorority have generally felt close to the Omegas, particularly as a group. They have been quite supportive of each other and there have been more than a random number of marriages of Omegas and Deltas, I observe, especially when they come from different campuses.

I have given a number of talks before groups of Greeks during my tenure. Usually these have emphasized the value of Panhellenism, Greeks pulling together to provide role models for the rest of the campus and the community, that deficiencies and misconduct on the part of any Greek detracts from the influence of all Greeks. I have stressed scholarship and service, really the two features which distinguish Greeks as a group.

But this group was different. It was made up of young women who were initiated from around 1974 through 1989. The range of achievements and possibilities among them was noticeable. The oldest of them were not yet 40 years old and are in the flower of their womanhood. When I looked around and discovered that I was the only male present, aside from one who was married to a Delta, I felt extra special. When it was my time to speak, after some music and talk by one of the founding lines of the chapter, I began to choke up. I almost wanted to cry. I was so happy. The fruits of all my years of college teaching and counseling were now being seen. It all seemed worth it. The girls and more mature sorors seemed so secure, impressive, human, I would say. They had matured beautifully and have grown into the type of women that any father would be happy for his daughter to be. I told them how proud I was of their taking their vows to the sorority seriously and living them out in their daily lives.

They chuckled when I told them how "unpromising" many of them were 16 years ago, how we as faculty members often shook our heads and despaired of their likelihood of getting themselves together to make something out of themselves. And I told them that is how most of us looked at that age. The Greek societies helped to mold them into what they are today. Some felt that they have no purpose to serve, that their records are such that they are no longer assets to the campuses or to the communities in which they are found. It is clear that around the country there have been troubles with certain chapters of Greeks, but a blanket indictment of them is a questionable conclusion. I believe that a Greek society can and does help many youths who would be unable to discover their own potential, as perhaps I myself would have gotten much less out of collegiate life had I not joined a Greek society. I ended up reminding them that after 40 years I am not sorry that I went Greek and if they continue to progress, deport themselves, and serve their communities according to the requirements of their societies, they will be able to say the same when their societies invite them back years later to reflect on the meaning of Greekdom in their lives.

13

Self Evaluation

What has been the real meaning of the fraternity as one looks backward over some 40 years of membership? It is not an unreasonable question. Is it possible that it will take its place in our memories as simply another secondary association, or was its meaning much deeper? In the language of sociology, for any secondary group to be meaningful it must be broken down into primary groups. The secondary group is too formal, too impersonal, too well organized. People relate to each other in terms of their ranks. But in primary groups people relate to each other because they like them. They have no particular agenda to carry out, they are not trying to achieve anything in particular. They simply enjoy the company and association of each other.

On one level Omega Psi Phi is a secondary group made up of thousands of men, supposedly of like belief. They represent all walks of life and virtually all cultures. They have varying beliefs and experiences. In a word, no two Ques are alike. It is hoped that they are tied together more by their ideals than by the likeness which comes from daily association. There is, consequently, no uniform yardstick by which the brothers may be measured for after they have taken it upon themselves to conduct their lives by the values set by the Founders there is little formal action the Fraternity may take against them if they fail to live up to those values. There are cases where brotherhood has been denied because of the actions of some brother. Most often the brother who feels he has betrayed the values of the Fraternity willfully withdraws and no longer associates himself with the group. In very few cases has the fraternity taken action against a brother, an action which amounts to excommunication. And a few brothers become disillusioned with the direction the fraternity has taken and dissociate themselves therefrom by returning all pins and certificates of membership.

I believe that each brother is best fitted to evaluate whether or not he is meeting the standards which the Fraternity has set. This evaluation may be a continuous one whose results may be considered personal. When someone joins the Omegas it is thought of as a lifetime commitment to the values of the Fraternity. A few persons may feel after a while that that commitment was too much and that membership was an expedient they wanted to exercise for a particular time or place. But the longer one remains within the group the greater the opportunity, and even the necessity, for evaluating oneself according to the demands of the Cardinal Principles. A 40 year benchmark would appear to be a good place for this evaluation to take place. At that stage one might be relatively satisfied that whatever pattern he was going to exhibit has had a good opportunity to become established. A 40 year brother is closing in on 60 years of age, if initiated around age 20. His view of the past is long enough to see many of the turns in the road, to understand his own potential, to have become set in whatever line of work he chose. Family obligations might be diminishing, or they might be increasing because of the presence of grandchildren. In a few short years he may be looking toward retirement, and in some cases that has already occurred. He still may think of the future but does so in terms quite different from those utilized 40 years ago when he was a much younger man. Much has changed in his life and some of these have affected the way he looks at all aspects of life, including the Fraternity.

An Omega self evaluation is not out of the realm of possibility or reality. We are evaluated constantly in almost all that we do. Unless we are self-employed we are evaluated by our employers who have yardsticks by which to measure our performance as well as our attitudes. Laying out the Cardinal Principles and trying to see whether we measure up to them does not seem to be too strange.

So what have I done during my 57 years as an Omega man which will bear scrutiny? Let's begin with the first principle: Manhood. I have tried to act the part of a man by carrying myself as such. I have stood up for what I thought was right and I have tried to meet all of my legitimate obligations--financial or social. I have done what I could to try to demonstrate that people respect you much more when you stand by your principles. I have not carried a sign to prove or announce to others that I am a man. People would know that by the way I acted. Anything which demeaned and took from the perception of the strength of manhood, I have rejected. Even during the days of racial discrimination I tried to carry myself in such a way that even those who would discriminate would think again. I wanted my name to stand for something: fairness, honesty, and strength of conviction. It was not necessary to humiliate others or be humiliated oneself.

Men have obligations which they do not try to shirk. I hope one of the best criteria of my manhood was my effort to hold my family together so that they could have some security and respect. This meant working long years at my profession, oftentimes without adequate remuneration or recognition. Trying to offer guidance to them at a time when the many distractions challenged my patience and sometimes my resolve that what I was doing was the right thing. Strength was required to continue under some of the handicaps which were faced which were not of my own doing. Some men have become so beaten down by the rigid requirements for respectability that they have dissolved their families or put distance between themselves and their family members. My wife and I have celebrated 50 years of marriage. We have had very rough spots but we have not fought, threatened divorce, or behaved in ways which cast aspersion upon the family. Our children have very little for which to be ashamed. We provided for them as best as we could. As parents we worked together as a team. I hope that some of what we accomplished was due, at least in part, to my trying to stand up and be counted as a man. But everyone can do a little better for none is perfect. On a scale of 10 on manhood I will give myself an eight.

What about scholarship? I have always enjoyed finding out more than I know, and that is what I call scholarship. Working in the academic field, in higher education, has meant that I had to do a certain amount of publishing of scholarly papers in order to keep credibility in my department and, literally, to keep a job. But even before I entered collegiate teaching, I had been interested in things scholastic. Most of the materials I have written have not been published, but here are a few things that some brothers or others may find interesting.

2007 *No Violence Is Progress*. A novel about integration of a Southern university. It was published 50 years after its writing. New York publishers thought it too hot for the South.

1967 *African Vignettes: Notes of an American Negro Family in East Africa*. While working in that section for two years it almost cost me my job with Teachers College, Columbia University, to maintain notes of my experiences there.

1970 *The Ghetto College Student*. A monograph on college students from the inner city.

1972 *Black Hillbillies of the Arkansas Ozarks*. An observational study of black people of the Ozarks Mountains.

1980 *America without Ethnicity*. A book seeking to understand the future of America without one of its major social problems.

1985 *Lawrence A. Davis: Arkansas Educator*. Brother Lawrence A. Davis, was a longtime president of Arkansas AM&N College, Pine Bluff, Arkansas.

1990 *The Edge of the Campus*. Forty years of blacks at the University of Arkansas.

These are not the only books I have written. I have not included textbooks in general sociology, East Africa, prisons, and novels on plantations and on the social life of George Washington Carver. I think the total number of books I have written, published and unpublished, is around 40. This does not include more than 30 journal articles and many feature stories and letters to editors.

I have not made much money as a scholar, but I have enjoyed every minute of it. On the dimension of scholarship I think I should have a 9 on a 10 point scale.

Have I tried to encourage the people who needed it badly, a category which includes many black people? In the vernacular of the Cardinal Principles we call this Uplift. The assumption was, when the Fraternity was founded, and even before, that black people needed to help each other. We faced discrimination commonly and it made good sense that we would need to pull ourselves out of it by collective effort. Booker T. Washington called it self-help, letting our buckets down where we were, making our little part of the desert blossom. We did not have access to all that the society offered, but neither did white society have access to that part which you controlled. It had to give up something to keep separated from blacks just as blacks had to give up something to be denied white fraternity. Some might have gained. The idea of parallel development drove America from before the Plessy decision until at least 1954. In a very technical sense we could do whatever we wanted to do with our ghetto so long as we did not cost whites much money and we did not want to spill out of the ghetto over into their preserves.

This was a good opportunity for us to use our talent in the development of our own communities for it meant we would not spend time worrying about what white folks had and feeling deprived because we did not have the same. As in Europe, Switzerland's success and prosperity, for example, should be no cause for alarm by Germans. They could do the same, if they put their minds to it, so the parallel development argument ran. People could use their talent and resources as they chose. If they did not develop their communities it was their own fault. In the U.S. blacks did not begin with equal resources but they could make much of what they had. They need not be a total burden on the general community. If their minds were as good as whites, as they claimed they were, they could build institutions which were the envy of the world. They would not have to rely on whites for approval. Uplift meant helping blacks to understand the meaning of self-help. It was understood that some of them, even many, had been beaten down by the system of oppression and uplift meant assisting them to recover their dignity and self-respect so that they might be returned to competitive trim.

I believe I have tried as hard as I knew how to communicate by word and example the meaning of uplift. I worked with youth, as a scoutmaster, teacher, Sunday School teacher. During my years of counseling students who thought they had no ability has been one of my continuing tasks. Trying to challenge blacks to live so that they would gain self-respect and then group and wider respect has been part of my life. The extent to which I have been successful in my efforts remains to be evaluated, but for now I feel that I have not been most deficient in assisting wherever I could to bring about more favorable position for black people. I give myself a seven.

Perseverance is also hard to evaluate. It is a personal quality. Life itself is one of perseverance or sticking to the goals one feels are worthwhile and acceptable. I have not gotten everything I wanted. Nor has what little I have gained been achieved without effort and anxiety. Let's use an example which many brothers faced, that of remaining in college in order to get degrees and meet the value of scholarship. For many months I was unsure from where my room and board would come. My father did not have a remunerative job. There were other children in the family. We had only a few years ago become convinced that security of a sort lay in home ownership.

If he did not want to have his life cut short my father would have to find a way of reducing the burden and tension. Rent had always been a problem. My father bought an old house during World War II, which took until the end of the war to pay off. Before we were clear with it, repairs needed to be made, plumbing installed, two rooms added so that the two girls and two boys could have rooms. Formerly, we all slept in one room for the house had only four rooms.

The last payment on the house had not been made when we were plunged into debt again, this time to purchase a 15 acre plot of land just outside the city limits. It had an old house which had never been painted. It had no plumbing. By then we were in high school and my brother getting ready for college. We had to learn perseverance while practicing it.

Getting a college degree with practically no money was evidence that I could hang tough. I will not talk about how many days I went hungry at the campus. There were some but not that many mainly because I had a meal ticket and a dormitory room. I had bought a suit from a frat brother for $10 and that kept me from looking too bad when we had to dress up on campus. I started to quit pledging when I did not have a tuxedo but my line brothers told me to persevere, which I did and borrowed a tuxedo from the president of the college, Bro. Lawrence A. Davis.

Getting a master's degree was not easy. There was some discouragement along the way in the form of low grades, the same as was the case with getting a doctorate. What I learned from the idea of perseverance was that one must "hang in there." So hanging tough became something I am proud to say has been one of my strong points. Buying homes which I thought I would never pay for, sending my children to college without financial aid, and continuing to fight for the things for which I believe, I hope are evidence of my persistence. Bro. Ariel M. Lovelace, a man whom I deeply admired as a youth, told a friend of his once, as he was making up the roster for his traveling choir, "That Morgan kid has the skin of an elephant. He just won't quit." He did not know how much that compliment meant to me. I think it says something for my internalization of the concept perseverance. I don't think I overrate myself by awarding myself a seven.

Overall, I feel that my work as a representative of Omega Psi Phi is honorable and I am not ashamed of the record I have made in living up to the ideals of the fraternity.

14

Pledging Rules from the Moratorium

It had become clear by about 1977, only three years after the founding of the chapter, that the potential existed for activities of the chapter to get out of hand. This was attributed mainly to a lack of adult supervision. No survey has been taken to determine how widespread the negative activities of the chapters were, but there is a strong suspicion that they were similar in a wide enough context for all to become disturbed.

A part of the problem of hazing goes back to tradition. Where toughness has become established in a chapter in order that the pledges show manhood, the tendency is to escalate the activities required of pledges There has long been fear within black organizations that there be no persons whose gender was ambiguous. It was especially strong within the ranks of the Omegas. That each pledge showed the normal evidence of masculinity was required. If a pledge had a girlfriend which was observable to everyone he ordinarily met the criterion. Pledges without girlfriends, and those too bookish or effeminate appearing were put through exceptionally rugged tests mainly to determine if they were abnormal or simply late in developing. Some pledges were too shy or too status conscious to try to make it with girls on campus and often they had to be encouraged. It was part of the Omega image, it was thought, to have normal relationships with members of the opposite sex. There was understandable concern with those who did not.

There was not much of a problem on the black campus. The ratio of girls to boys was about even, if not in favor of the boys. The boy could be relatively selective given this surplus of females. He may not like the selection but it was there for him to choose and there was no reason for any reasonably equipped male to do without female association. Of course, the campus was not the only option. Quite a few pledges came to college with girlfriends from high school, or they could be in other towns or schools. The main problem was to make sure that the pledge showed all of the characteristics of brothers with a normal interest in members of the opposite sex.

Of the very few cases I have seen of men who were denied entry into the pledge club, the reasons fell into a small number of categories. The first was grade-point-average (GPA). This objective criterion could easily be checked by the registrar. In the black college the group let the word circulate that letters were being received for the pledge club. When enough letters had come forward by a certain date the list of names was taken to the registrar who would list their GPAs, majors, and credit hours. If a person did not have the GPA to meet school requirements, the registrar so indicated. The chapter could be suspended if it pledged anyone who was short of school GPA requirements.

The second major stumbling block to getting into the Pledge Club was anything which could be considered a serious character defect. Certain eccentricities were permitted for it was understood that persons were different and had a variety of interests. Musicians and performing artists, for instance, could have some temperaments for that was thought to be their nature. Natural science majors could be expected to be coldly practical, more hardheaded than social science majors. The one thing which was not permitted was a deviation from interest in the opposite sex. If a pledge were interested only in himself this was frowned upon. It could go against his admission into the Pledge Club and could be a continuing problem before and after his entry into the fraternity. It was thought best to keep out of the Lampados Club all persons whose manhood seemed in doubt.

Poverty could be a problem to some pledges. The financial hardships of black students in the decades before the 1970s were well known. If a chapter wanted a brother who had a legitimate financial hardship they have been known to find ways, washing cars, providing work for the brother, and even signing bank loans to assist the prospective brother. In the vast majority of cases the interest of individual brothers or the chapter in a prospective brother has not been misused.

But perhaps those were norms more in vogue when the fraternity was much younger. They seemed to have been the case when I was initiated fifty-seven years ago. Things change and the attitudes of pledges toward the nature of fraternity and the meanings of its ideals may have undergone some modification. It has been much harder to keep the young men headed in the direction the founders intended. In some cases the movement has been so far away from the ideals that new organizations have been formed. The BIG EIGHT: Alpha Phi Alpha, Kappa Alpha Psi, Phi Beta Sigma, and Omega Psi Phi (fraternities) and Alpha Kappa Alpha, Delta Sigma Theta, Sigma Gamma Rho, and Zeta Phi Beta (sororities) no longer have clear monopolies on the Greek aspirations of black youth. In addition to some joining majority organizations, other black organizations have formed on the national level primarily, we believe, because of their disenchantment with the activities and examples set by the older societies. The issue of pledging is certainly one of the main factors giving rise to the growth of additional organizations. The following set of rules were suggested to help a chapter deal with its pledging problems. It is not much in evidence that they were adopted by the chapter.

PLEDGE RULES FOR LAMPADOS CLUB

Time and Place of Meetings and Obligations

1. A pledgee shall be obligated to the Chapter for no more than two hours per week during the pledge period (then 8-10 weeks).
2. No meeting of the pledge group shall be longer than two hours.
3. Pledge meetings may be called by order of the Dean of Pledgees and, with his consent, by his designated assistant.
4. Pledgees may call a meeting when they choose when the same does not conflict with those called by the Chapter.
5. Meetings of the pledge club by the Chapter will be held at a regularly scheduled time and place which will be known to the Chapter and its advisor(s).

6. No pledging of the Lampados Club will take place unless there are two-thirds of bona fide Chapter members present.

Recognition of Big Brothers

7. No pledge is required to recognize a brother who is not in good standing with the Chapter.
8. Pledges are required to show ordinary courtesies to visiting brothers who present themselves as bona fide and in good standing with their chapters.
9. A pledgee is obligated to recognize a Big Brother in normal activity.
10. A pledgee is not obligated to recognize a brother functioning in a role other than one associated with the Fraternity; for example, if a pledge is a teacher (teaching assistant, graduate assistant, etc.) and the Big Brother a student, the pledgee need not defer to the student while he is in his teacher role.
11. Uniformed pledgees are to maintain the decorum required of them while in uniform.
12. No pledgee is obligated to recognize a brother at a significant financial, time, or psychological cost to himself.
13. A pledgee is required to show normal courtesies to Big Brothers when visiting other campuses.

Physical Tests, Work and Money

14. A pledgee is not required to submit to any form of paddling, pinching, pushing, posturing, or other physical hazing.
15. Pledgees are required to indicate to the Dean of Pledgees any physical or medical condition which may interfere with pledge activities. No pledgee is required to perform any activity which is dangerous or which he is physically limited to perform.
16. No pledgee is obligated to do demeaning work or to carry out any illegal activity for any brother.
17. No pledge is obligated to undertake any work for any brother for which pay is ordinarily given unless this is on an arrangement of business or personal friendship.

Pledging Rules 89

18. No pledge is required to lend money to any brother. Personal friendships are excepted.
19. Pledgees are not required to raise funds for the Chapter. Any funds raised will be maintained by the Pledge Club and used for acceptable purposes.

General

20. A pledgee must be given reasonable time to fulfill a task.
21. Pledge work shall not be in conflict with the usual obligations of the pledgees-athletics, work, studies, or other activities by which the pledgee is making his living or trying to live up to the values of the Fraternity. Pledgees are to be provided with the names, addresses, phone numbers, and status (graduate, undergraduate, active or inactive), of all brothers in the immediate area.
22. Pledgees are to wear no Fraternity symbols or insignia aside from the Lampados Pin during the pledge period.
23. As many meetings as are required shall be used to familiarize pledgees with these rules.

These rules are placed in effect for the purposes of having pledgees understand their rights and obligations to the Fraternity during the pledge period and for the general protection of pledgees, the Fraternity, and its sponsors. Each pledgee is to be provided a set of these rules.

Signed (Chapter members)

15

Achievement Day Banquet Address

Omega Psi Phi Fraternity, Inc.
Wichita, Kansas
November 13, 1993

To the members of the head table, the officers and brothers of this great Fraternity, and to those friends of our Fraternity who have come here today to help us celebrate the achievements of the fraternity, not only for the year, but for some years past, I am deeply honored to appear before you as your speaker. I do thank very kindly Brother Prentic Henry, who helped initiate me into the fraternity forty-three years ago. He also initiated my brother a year earlier. I don't know how senior that makes him. We have enjoyed friendship lo these many years.

The theme for this occasion is on the importance and salvation of the black male, which some have called an endangered specie. This is an extremely timely subject and one which is critical to the continuity of the black family, the backbone of black society. Some brothers have already informed you that the Fraternity was begun formally in 1911 and incorporated in 1914 as a union or conclave of men, most of them then young, who saw a vision and a need for a brotherhood which stressed the principles of manhood, scholarship, uplift, and perseverance. These terms have been well defined, but for emphasis let me repeat their meaning. I shall elaborate most upon the meaning of Manhood, around which this theme is built. The other cardinal, or outstanding principles, Scholarship, Perseverance, and Uplift, really shade over, and are included in the basic one of manhood.

Scholarship means, not so much getting good grades in school, but means a lifelong cultivation of the mind through the medium of reading, thinking and reflecting, in the manner reminiscent of scholars of the middle age. Perseverance means not quitting, hanging in there against obstructions, hardships and discouragement.

Uplift means doing something positive for those who are in less fortunate positions than ourselves. It sounds a little bit noblesse oblige, but it is still necessary for those a bit more able to do a bit more, to shoulder more of the load for the improvement of all.

Manhood means doing those things which men do. In the present context, it seems that manhood is ambiguous, that in some cases it is confused with something else. We believe manhood means the protection of our families, the caring for our children, the standing for something positive. It means standing for fair play and correct treatment for all regardless of station in life. It is not thought of as being equated with the image of the supermasculine menial elaborated in Eldridge Cleaver's book *Soul on Ice*. It does not mean taking advantage of all the girls in town, like *BAD BAD LEROY BROWN*.

There are people today who are trying to confuse the meaning of manhood with other statuses in life. For example, the breakthroughs in science have made us aware of the similarities between males and females. We know that on the basis of anatomy alone, that is, what the physical facts of biology tell us, there is no great difference between males and females. Some females are stronger than males; some females are brighter than males; some females make much better decisions than males. Being a male is a matter of biology, but being a man is a matter of sociology. Being a female is a matter of biology, but being a woman is a matter of sociology. This means that we must be assigned our gender roles; we must learn them in a social context. Ordinarily, boys will learn to be boys and girls to be girls. Ordinarily, young boys will grow into manhood and girls into womanhood. However, if there is some degree of confusion, it will be possible for boys to not fully understand what maleness is and later manhood. It is our contention, backed up by data and common sense, that boys must be taught to be men in the same way that we learn many other roles. It does not come naturally. Nothing which is a social reality comes naturally.

When this fraternity was founded, the strong belief was that manhood had to be taught, cultivated, seen as an example. There were many things which were being done which males did but which were not manly. A male might use his superior strength to overwhelm a woman, rob her, violate her, but that is not manly behavior. A great sociologist once said that without social training we would remain like the animals, behaving according to the very basest urges which define and determine animal behavior. The black male is of particular interest to the society of today. It is not necessary that we rehearse the dismal statistics regarding the failure of our young men to be all that they can be, that is, in a positive way. We know all too well how many of them are in prison, in drug use, in gangs, and doing poorly in schools. The question for us is to understand why this is so. Everyone has his or her reasons. These range from the place of the home in the instilling of values of right and wrong and of fair play. Some say that the school is not informing the young Afro–American male of the necessity of playing the game within the well established rules, that the real purpose of the schools is to miseducate the black male so that he will not become a force in his own welfare, nor of the welfare of his family. Role models are held up to the Afro–male that are really unrealistic. The young male learns early to aspire to the big money which comes from outside instead of through traditional development.

Let me now talk for a moment about one of the movements aimed at strengthening the image and self–concept of the African American male. It is called the Academy Movement. Not all will agree with what it proposes to do. But because of the critical problem facing black males, it is absolutely essential that some steps be taken to redress the problem.

The Black Academy Movement

The Black Academy Movement has become a movement ostensibly aimed at the improvement of the academic performance of black males. In certain cities schools have been set aside for black males, mainly under high school age, for the purpose of giving them the instruction which they are said not to get in the public schools. In the larger cities where the problems of the public schools are most noticeable, more difficult to solve, the discouraging statistics on black male lack of achievement promote a number of strategies for educational improvement, of which the Black Academy is one.

Inner city schools, now noted for their atmospheres which discourage academic achievement, are being abandoned by the middle class elements who are fleeing to suburbs and schools where their children may have a better chance at receiving a quality education. In many cases parents are paying fees equivalent to or in excess of those paid for college tuition for their elementary schoolage children to attend prestigious schools assumed to be of high quality. Parents unable to afford the high fees and who cannot afford to leave the inner city, are left with the alternative of trying to improve the inner city schools. They press for everything from curriculum revision to the emplacement in the schools of teachers and administrators of the same ethnicity as the children. Middle class strategies to avoid the educational problems of the inner city ghetto, include pressing for vouchers to enable them to spend their educational dollar where they choose. The magnet school is one which places high scoring students of common interest in the same school thereby excusing them from association with the students from the ghetto.

With the decline of busing to achieve ethnic balance the schools are becoming more and more single ethnicity schools. Inner city schools are becoming more isolated, volatile, and alienated from the general educational system. The signs are present that these schools mean less to the larger community than they ever did, because of the multiplicity of problems found in them. A consequence of the isolation of the inner city schools is the attempt of parents to propose strategies which will take their children out of the public school environment. Because of the many problems facing the black male it has been thought that more must be done to salvage these youth from lives of destruction.

The Philosophy of the Black Male Academy

The black male academy is founded upon the colonialist principle that the local environment in which the student lives is antithetical to his academic and intellectual development. It was an assumption drawn by missionaries and anthropologists who felt that to convert native children to European, civilized, ways it was necessary to take them out of the local environment.

The boarding school served that purpose for it separated the children from their parents and community and in time taught them that they were superior to their environments. Leaders of the boarding school idea argued that they had to have virtually complete control over the students if students were to hang on to the advantages they gained at school. Their home environments were not good ways of reinforcing the teachings of the schools for fundamentally these two teachings were in disagreement. Practically every aspect of the life of the child would need to be overhauled if that child hoped to fit into a credible European mold. Literally the parents would turn the child over to the boarding school authorities who would mold the child to the expectations of the European community. It was neither possible nor desirable to convert too many native children to European values and so only a few of the most highly promising ones were selected. A major means of reducing the number was the charging of fees beyond the abilities of the majority of parents to pay. Head Start was a program based upon the unequal distribution of opportunity between poor and better off communities. Basically, in Head Start, poor children received the same opportunity to be taught the same values as those of the larger community. It sought to equalize opportunity by working with children, parents, and the community. The model used were symbols of middle class success, from table manners to total socialization.

Head Start was also founded on the assumption that there were cultural differences between poor and middle class communities which differences translated into cultural deficits. The deficits of the poor children could be overcome by management of their curriculum and environment. Often the curriculum was enriched to include much assumed available to children of the middle class. After more than twenty years it was found that Head Start did not deliver the positive benefits envisioned. A secondary premise of Head Start was that poor children were raised under conditions of repression, especially parental.

A child was too greatly inhibited to achieve much. Overcoming that inhibition was a requirement for success. Accordingly, certain words such as "No, don't do that," and others which served to place limits on the behavior of the child were banned as handicaps to the full development of the child. Financing of the black male academy provided the same problem as was faced in the boarding school colonial context.

In Arkansas we have the case of some six boys named Chambers. They lived in the delta, or the cotton farming section of the state, along the Mississippi River. Their parents had been sharecroppers much earlier, but by about 1950, the plantation system was all but gone. The family had to move to the city of Marianna where they had no way of making a living except by day work. The father became demoralized and left the family. The mother could not control the boys and at school, even under the leadership of a very prominent educator, they found that education was not their way out of poverty. They drifted first to Memphis and then to Detroit where they began to traffic in drugs. At first the oldest boy went to Detroit, then each of the younger boys came as he became old enough. In a few years these boys, the Chambers Boys, were living high in the city. Everybody knew them for their drug dealings. They had wads of money. They came back to Marianna to attend a high school graduation of some of their relatives. They were in a fleet of rented white Cadillacs and so captured the imaginations of the younger children that the school people had trouble restraining the youngsters, many of whom understood that the way to go was through participation in the drug traffic. All of the Chambers Boys are now in the penitentiary for long sentences, and one has already passed away. But drugs are not the only way to believe that one can reach fame and fortune.

Prominent scholars claim that the black middle class has left the black community, moving to the suburbs where their interest in the community is no longer. That is no doubt true. The old middle class is gone leaving no one except public workers of charity in the community. Even these people leave the community at the five o'clock bell. In almost any city, now surrounding the black community, it is vacant after sundown for everyone has headed to the suburbs. Who is left to lead the black community? Who has responsibility for it? We, of course, cannot go back to the days when the black middle class controlled the community mostly through its moral force. We cannot go back to the days when the chief of police called the principal of the colored school, as it was called in those days, and said, I have one of your students down here. He stole something from one of the ten cents stores. What do you want me to do with him? Very often the principal would say give me a few minutes and I will be down there. Down at the chief's office the principal would say, "Let me have him and I'll see that he is not in trouble anymore." The principal would lecture the youth sternly, or even go to his parents and tell them what the youth had to do to stay out of the reform school. The youth would understand very clearly that he had to obey the principal and all the teachers, the preachers, doctors, businessmen on the colored side of town as it was then called, old people, and all others who had any degree of respect and standing in the community. If the youth could not conform his behavior to community expectations, he was gone. It was as simple as that. The leaders of the community thought that the best way to achieve rights was by demonstrating that we were in control of our own community, that it was the best place to live, that our children were the best mannered, that they could be compared with the very best that the majority community could put up. All we needed was a chance. We would not bring embarrassment to ourselves, to our families, or to our communities.

There was a total network of control and there was a relatively low crime rate. The black community was safe enough for almost anybody who wanted to walk the streets. Then there was a great amount of pride in black communities. We competed against each other in the big games. In big cities games between say, Froebel High School of Gary, Indiana, and Booker T. Washington High, of Chicago, were bigger than two teams meeting on the playing field or basketball court. They were symbols of the bonding of communities. Sometimes there were very serious pranks, but basically authorities expected the leaders of the schools and communities to control the fans, and they usually did. These were tension releasing means which, at the same time, gave the people something to look forward to. Some of that pride still exists, but it is obviously not as strong as it was once upon a time. We cannot leave the topic of the black male without talking about the issue of role models. The thought makers and brokers have placed before young males models which are perhaps inappropriate. And these are no longer the athletic and entertainment stars of the past. They are the generals of gangland.

In a recent 60 Minutes show a book written by a young man now serving some seven years for a variety of crimes, tells his story of crime from the early years. He says that crime was the same as going to college or engaging in any other regular endeavor. It was something that all the youth were doing and if one did not do it he was square. One had to work his way up through the network as is commonly the case in organizational setting. To be the best gang-leader was the height of his ambition. It was not something that he had a lot of choice over. The sale of this book by this bright young black male continues the tradition of glamorization of negative role models. It is expected to sell more than a quarter million copies. I believe its title is *Monster. Sanyika Shakur Monster: The Autobiography of an L.A. Gang Member* (New York: Penguin , 1993).

The problem, of course, is not the book itself. We certainly wish the author every success in having his message told. It is unfortunate, though, that a young man must go through all the problems that Monsta has gone through, killing, robbing, stealing, descending to the very lowest level of humanity, ending up in jail and barely avoiding the electric chair or the cyanide pellets. What is the reason that we were unable to reach him, and many others like him? What has happened to the black community. This youth did not even grow up in what is typically thought of as the ghetto. Although his parents were not together, he does not seem to have suffered all that much; he was never deprived, and did not have to fend for himself. He states, though that it was the streets which had a greater appeal than legitimate avenues to success. When this young man gets out of prison he will have a quarter million dollars waiting for him, which will be encouragement for other young people to follow the same trail. What Afro male who has traveled the regular route, gone to school, got a job, supported his family, and tried to stand for something positive in his community will be favored with a best selling book and movie rights? Is there a payoff for deviance which is greater than that for behaving oneself?

Yes, the problem of the young black male is with us. It will remain the duty of our community to bring this young man back to usefulness in the community. We cannot look for others, whether government or other social institutions to do it. That is one of the reasons this fraternity was founded, to make sure that young men in a brotherhood, with positive plans and guidance and instruction, could come together, to discuss, to plan and to conduct their lives in such a way that they would be a credit to all who had the privilege of knowing them.

It has indeed been my pleasure to speak to you this evening.

16

Que Finals

Fifty years is a long time any way it is approached. It is long enough to cycle through most of the important phases of life and to have time to reflect on what has been accomplished, or even attempted. Many of the persons who were our close friends have deceased or perhaps we have not seen them for many years. They were doing what they could to make pleasant lives for themselves and their families. Many are no doubt still doing it. Everything has changed and we have changed and continue to do so and our relationship to the events and changes are certainly not what they were that many years ago. Moments of reflection on it all are both useful and therapeutic.

What can we say which will be of benefit to young brothers which will cause older brothers, or even their friends, to read and say "Brother So-and-So is alright?" That is the hard part. I guess it may not be so harmful to get personal at this point in my life. More than 40 years ago we were in our cramped dormitory rooms at Arkansas AM&N College, as it was then called, talking about the future, how we would make our marks, and what the odds were, given the problems we faced. I must digress a bit while talking about change. The old school of which I discuss as the setting in which I became an Omega Man began in 1875 by a man who had the same ideas then as we had in the late 1940s and hopefully have today. Joseph C. Corbin, the school founder would have been a man who would have been a credit to either of the Greek societies. He exemplified the Omega Psi Phi principles of scholarship, manhood, perseverance, and uplift. The school was called Branch Normal for it was a branch of the University of Arkansas. In 1928 it was changed to the Agricultural, Mechanical and Normal College and separated from the University. In 1971, or so, it was changed again to the University of Arkansas at Pine Bluff and reintegrated into the University System.

When I was initiated into the fraternity in 1950, there had not yet been a Brown decision allowing us to attend, teach or work in schools and institutions not separated from the mainstream. Although most students did work their way through college, there was no formal work study program. It had to be bootlegged by the president in the form of reducing the costs of the college by having students perform much of the work required to keep it operating. There was no such thing as Affirmative Action to help us get a few chances when there were so many determined to see us fail. There had only recently been the desegregation of the military services. Only a few black schools had Reserve Officer Training Programs and the majority of us who would enter military service would do so as enlisted men, unless we were specially talented or trained in high demand technical areas. Almost everywhere, but especially in the South, our options were limited.

But even then there was no room for despair. Our leaders, especially our professors and teachers, tried to give us the confidence they knew we needed for there were so many opportunities to become demoralized. We knew we would make it and do alright. It was a matter of having the right stuff which meant an attitude toward success more than anything else. The trick was to keep focused, stick to your knitting, learn all you could, sty out of trouble, and not give up, even when the hour looked darkest. There were many ways of challenging the system, something we all learned. Every commander knew that a frontal assault was not always the best plan of attack for every target.

The fraternity was very helpful toward keeping us focused. The formal meetings were just that – formal. That is not where we got the inspiration. It was in those informal sessions, in rooms on weekends, at the campus deli where there were gatherings of students on weekends and Sundays, for we did not yet have a student union building, coming and going to class when opportunities presented themselves to talk without any agenda. It was playing intramural sports as a group. It was sharing food and clothes and occasionally money with a friend, sometimes not even a fraternity brother. It was after those long, knock-down and drag-out meetings we had when we made all right with each other by locking arms and marching around the campus, ending up at the girls' dormitories and singing those close harmony songs in the still of the delta night, songs which brought the girls to their windows and tears to their eyes. It was by having to attend convocations during which "role models," persons whom we were very likely to respect for their having overcome great odds to make enviable names for themselves, told us how they had overcome, and how we could do the same. Perhaps as much as anything we learned that all of us were in the same fraternity. The symbols we wore, whether Alpha Phi Alpha, Kappa Alpha Psi, Phi Beta Sigma, or Omega Psi Phi, were more like designations of units in the military service. And that fraternity was not limited to men. Women were a part of it, and their symbols, Alpha Kappa Alpha, Sigma Gamma Rho, Zeta Phi Beta and Delta Sigma Theta, allowed them full participation in the struggle which we all knew we faced. We were all dedicated to the propositions of building a viable black community by encouraging everyone to be all positive that he or she could be.

It would all be reenacted years later, even in our minds, as we returned to the campus, often gray, paunchy, bald, grandparents, still trying to assess our success and to impress on the younger generation the importance of staying in the struggle. We would meet old friends and relive old times, not knowing how many more times this would happen. Next year may be too late. We may see young brothers wearing the symbols of our beloved fraternity and we would be happy. Perhaps we might even wear them ourselves. Most likely not, for we would know that the big fraternity claimed our attention. It may not be very meaningful what symbols one wore. And yet, there were stirrings of those boyhood ambitions, brought back by old friendships. We always remembered those who were before us.

Most of us could not remember when the chapter was brought to the campus. It seemed to have always been there by the time we were initiated. By my initiation a folklore had been built up surrounding the men who were Omega. They seemed to be everywhere, in all the important positions on the campus, in the town, in business, in the professions. Whether it was true or not, the impression was made that if one were an Omega Man, he was expected to be successful. Nothing less would do. It was not necessary to point only to the older men who were successful, though this was done often enough. Omega men who were college presidents seemed common enough. Benjamin Mays, of Morehouse, Albert Dent, Dillard, and Lawrence A. Davis, of AM&N College, were some of the more notable ones. There were plenty of younger people who served as inspiration to us.

At the national levels there were the Olympic track stars such as Reggie Pearman and Harrison Dillard and professional football greats such as Len Ford of the Cleveland Browns. On our own campus there were Eddie Mays and Fred Balenton and Harold Cowans in the top honor societies. Mallory "Tiger' Jones, Shelton McGhee, Harmon Hill, and Prentic Henry, literally running the choir by exercise of talent and organizational skill. On the teams Omega men were performing competently. In the laboratories, on the farm, wherever opportunities for growth presented themselves, there were bound to be Omega men involved. As young initiates we were happy to see brothers like James Theophilous Jones, president of the student body, literally preparing himself for a great career in politics. He later became professor of political science at Atlanta University. I am sure that the other organizations made the same impressions on their young initiates.

As we left campus we tried to carry that same attitude, the can do spirit, the determination to continue to exercise the principles of scholarship, perseverance, manhood, and uplift. They would become daily operating standards by which our own lives could be organized.

Any organization competes for the control of the lives of individuals involved. That is part of the indoctrination process. The deeper the indoctrination the longer it takes to extinguish. If there are reinforcements along the way the original indoctrination continues. I have had the opportunity of observing many Omega men and their commitment to the principles of the fraternity. Some become more involved the older they get and some less. The lessening of involvement is often more a function of physical limitations than of loss of interest. The older we get there is a greater realization that we try to meet the cardinal principles in ways different than we did when we were younger. We may be less able to engage in the physical activities which attract the younger brothers. We cannot stay up until the wee hours of the morning at some social function as we could years ago. If we are able financially we are more prone to meet the principles by writing a check. As we did four decades ago, though, we are still committed to the principles for which the fraternity stands. We still are thrilled when we see the young brothers trying, on the levels they can, to meet those principles.

17

The March of the Generations

It has now been over 50 years since I entered college and learned about Greek life. The role models that were placed before me still stand out in my mind: Lawrence A. Davis, president the college, Earl Ford, a close assistant, Sellars J. Parker, head of agriculture, Tilman C. Cothran, head of the department of sociology, Butler T. Henderson, of the department of business, Malvin E. Moore , Jr., head of the tailoring department, Harris, in mechanic arts, Marion C. George , a war hero and outstanding instructor in biology, Ariel M. Lovelace, head of the department of music, John M. Howard, head of the department of art, George G.M. James, the West Indian, a general all- around scholar, were just some of the men that we saw and looked up to. And on the student side there such outstanding students as Bobby Wayne Daniel, Nelson Talbot, Fred Balenton, Harold Cowan, Mallory Jones, Edward Mays, and Carl Brooks. Omegas seemed to be everywhere and in everything that seemed to count. There were Ques on all the teams, in student politics, in acting and drama, on the newspaper and yearbook staffs. And in the city of Pine Bluff there were professional men like Attorney W. Harold Flowers, medical doctors, dentists such as Bro. Willie Mollette, preachers such as. Dr. D.F. Martinez, and community school heads.

And there were counterparts in Alpha Phi Alpha, Kappa Alpha Psi, and Phi Beta Sigma. It was a good time to be Greek for there were so much fun, friendly competition, and much work to be done which we, in retrospect, plunged into eagerly.

It seemed that people pledged, were chosen, and initiated on the basis of promise. And once they got initiated we hoped they would live up to the standards set by the fraternity. Nobody wanted to let the fraternity down and so he was expected to live by a code which ensured respect for himself and thereby for the group.

Then building the fraternity was the same as building the black community. We were in the last phases of the era of separatism. It would be a very few years before the passing of the Brown Decision which would bring some change, but not enough and not fast enough. It would be a short time before Rosa Parks would not move in Montgomery, Alabama, and Martin Luther King, Jr. would be propelled to leadership in perhaps the greatest move for human equality America had ever seen. It would be a time when the overall system would be most hostile, though this time in legal ways, whereas formerly naked violence was used to halt black citizenship. Every man who had something to offer was expected to do so. The fraternity and sorority systems were means of helping toward those ends. This was a time of pulling together, perhaps more so than at any other time in the history of black Americans and no time for divisiveness. The struggle could not be slowed down by irrelevant considerations. It was a time when there was a reduced emphasis on naming who was doing what or who was a fraternity or sorority member. We were glad that our brothers were involved at all levels of the struggle but harmony was a most important necessity. There could be no divisiveness along the fissures of Greek and other social memberships.

The struggle for civil rights did not begin with Rosa Parks' failure to move nor did it end with the death of Martin Luther King, Jr., when he was shot in Memphis, Tennessee, in 1968. It took another form. And it still required initiative, brains, and determination to press on at the new levels. There were openings in the system of thought brought about by America's guilt over the mistreatment of some of her oldest citizens who had never received their full entitlements, guilt made so poignant by the symbolism of the death of King. Some blacks began to rise to high positions and move into secure middle class lifestyles. Many of these persons were college educated and being so were often Greek. They worked quietly in the systems in which they were found. And because of the changed nature of the struggle some thought they were working too slowly and only for personal benefits.

Naturally, accusations arose that there were blacks who had abandoned the struggle since they had made some personal achievements. No longer was it necessary to identify with the movement considered in the language of the fraternity as uplift. By the mid-1960s the issue had come to a head in the form of questioning who was really black. Some thought you were black only if you were in the movement and identified publicly with it. Mean concepts such as "oreo," a person black on the outside but white on the inside, came to the fore. The idea of the black bourgeoisie took on a new meaning from that given by E.F. Frazier in his famous book by that title. The old bourgeoisie were limited to the black community and worked hard to make it livable. The new bourgeoisie were often outside the community and did not have to rely upon it for either economic or social status. The NAACP would take care of cases of blatant discrimination against uneducated blacks and Affirmative Action would assure that qualified blacks were given equal opportunities. Would there be any need to use the Greek system as a means of social reform, some asked?

The responsibility of the educated blacks to the uneducated was discussed at high levels of bitterness. Nathan Hare could scold the brotherhood in a book entitled THE BLACK ANGLO SAXONS, suggesting that black people had, under the new freedoms, reached the goal they had wanted all the time, even when they were not aware of it, that of being white, or at least being treated with all their rights as though they were white. And by 1978 Bro. William Julius Wilson thought he recognized that race was declining in importance as a social force in American life. His *The Declining Significance of Race* forced many blacks of the educated class, a class which included many Greeks, to reconsider their responsibilities to the black community, if any at all remained. If the educated had no responsibility to the uneducated, the groups lower down in the opportunity structure, then the concept *Uplift* would have lost much of its meaning and so would the idea of fraternal cohesion for the purpose of advancing the group. Basically, what could the Greeks do for me, or I do for the community? This question posed a problem for the black Greeks as a result of the newly extended freedoms and opportunities. If community building was not the issue then black Greekdom would mean the same as it meant in the majority group. And it would cost less for there would not be the extra expense of houses to maintain.

By the mid-1990s black Greek chapters had been established on the campuses of majority campuses throughout the country. In many cases these chapters were founded and operated on the principles of those on the black campuses. Faculty members had usually attended or had some connection with those campuses and felt that black Greeks on the majority campuses would function largely as they knew they functioned on black campuses.

On the black campuses the Greek system was composed mainly of campus leaders and students outstanding in some phase of student life—academic or social. It was closely monitored to see that the members were behaving according to expectation and living by the rules of the institution. Although deans of men and women were the ones formally expected to oversee the behavior of the students, all faculty members were expected to assist in that role. The schools were small enough, with the majority of students living on campus, that all faculty members were basically supervisors of all students. The concept of in loco parentis operated at the black school no matter what the teaching level of that school. It was as operative in the colleges as in the lower schools, whether these were large city or small town schools. The campus is something like a family with members of that family feeling somewhat responsible for each other. If a student were exceptional in some area, the whole campus benefited and generally all were happy, even if the student were not a member of one's fraternity or sorority. Likewise, a student who fell on hard times or in social disfavor felt the disapproval of the entire campus.

Initiation into the Greek system was a process of indoctrination into the values of that system. There was to be both physical and emotional involvement in that indoctrination. It was a rare initiate who did not come to internalize the values of the organization, or at least to show the attitudes the members, and their advisors thought proper. Oftentimes youth changed very noticeably when they were faced with the pressures of indoctrination. For some this was the first time real social pressure had been placed on them. Many of the students attending the schools had come from desperate home and community situations, not merely conditions of poverty. Where they came from the large inner city ghettos, often with limitations on their behavior, the discipline of obeying rules set by others was something they had to work at doing. It was hard on some of the young men, but when they saw that the process was for their benefit, they usually did not object. Some of these brothers became the most supportive of the values of the fraternity once they were initiated.

When the black fraternities and sororities were established on the majority campuses, and they began to operate as they did on the black campuses, some began to call the indoctrination process hazing. Since the typical black Greek society did not have a house on the majority campus, and its activities had to be conducted almost publicly, all could see what it was doing, its social activities, and the behavior of the members toward the initiates. When they did get houses, their budgets could not afford house parents. Leadership of those houses had to be taken over mainly by older members, often students themselves who did not have the fullest support of the general membership. Basically, there was very little supervision of the black Greeks on the majority campus. Black faculty members, often very few in number, were spread very thinly in trying to manage, inspire, and supervise an increasingly large number of black student organizations and activities, all the while having to meet the academic production quotas imposed by their departments. For black Greeks much of the indoctrination process could not be controlled and some Greeks became overzealous. In some cases extremes were reached and lines had to be discontinued.

The Grand Chapter, or national organization, became aware of these problems and tried to deal with them as best as possible. On some black campuses, where there were changes in the mission of the schools, where scholars there had to become competitive with those in the majority schools, black faculty members could no longer devote the time to management of student groups. Hazing became as great at those schools as at the majority ones. The usual response of the Grand Chapter, with the concurrence of the institution, was to suspend the offending chapter for a certain period of time. The hope was that the members creating the problem would graduate or leave the campus and the youth more traditional would move in to fill the voids created.

It is at this crossroads that black Greeks today find themselves. Will their principles of black community improvement mean anything? Will service to that community become a bonding force among the Greeks? Or will they become identified as college youth trying to be somewhat differentiated from the rank and file of others mainly through the display of the symbols of wealth and parental social status.

And what about those of us who are now in the twilight of our careers whose children are now into their own careers? Those Greeks who were initiated in the 1930s or before now have grandchildren who are in college. Those initiated in the 1940s have children who are now in or even out of college. We do not know how many of the children or grandchildren continued the tradition begun in their families in 1906 with the founding of Alpha Phi Alpha or in 1911 with the founding of Omega Psi Phi, or others founded around the same times. I suppose nearly every parent who was Greek wants his or her child to choose the same organization as the parent chose. If they do the tradition is continued. If they do not they are still full members of the family. We know of families where very college student is a member of a different Greek society. And we know of cases where children "went different ways" for reasons other than their appreciation of the organizations they chose. Some want simply to spite their parents. And, sadly, some youth associate Greek membership with values they do not approve. It is not absolutely certain that our children will agree with us in what we believe in and for what we stand. It should not be wholly unexpected that they may not choose our Greek societies for they may feel that there is no place for them in the modern world.

Every parent, teacher, or leader of any sort, knows that it is extremely difficult to communicate across generations. Sometimes this communication is harder to achieve than that across rigid ranks. Even when we use the same words they do not mean the same. A child cannot know, or perhaps, will have difficulty in appreciating the meaning parents or adults attach to activities or values. Children are not clones of parents. Perhaps the only way that they will partially understand what things meant to parents is to become one themselves. But all would hope that their children saw something in their parents which they liked and which encouraged them to emulate their parents to some extent.

My father was not a college man but he had many qualities I

liked. Had he had the opportunity to attend college and pledge a fraternity, there is no doubt in my mind that he would have pledged Omega. He believed in the principles for which the group stands. He worked to support his family; he respected womanhood; he admired and sought learning; he was not easily discouraged and continued against strong opposition. And he did all he could to assist those less fortunate than himself for what we would today call group uplift. Isn't that what we call perseverance? He was a man of his word, standing for values of right and fair play. Isn't that what we call manhood?

We learn from those older than ourselves. Their experiences can be our teachers. As I learned from those whom I saw at home and at college, so did and do those who see me learn from me. I hope I am as impressive to some of the youth as some of my elders were to me. We do not always know who is observing us, not even our children. If we see signs that they would like to emulate our lives that is a tremendous testimony to their appreciation of us.

As early as 1975 my nephews began to attempt to pledge Omega. They were under no pressure to do so. Perhaps they saw something in my brother, their uncles, and myself that they liked. In 1980 my older son decided to pledge. That line was discontinued by national chapter order. In 1985 my second son pledged and was initiated. That was a very happy day in my life. During the initiation he took the ritual like a man. I wanted to run to his aid for the urge of fatherhood was so strong that when I saw my son being pushed beyond the bounds of necessity, I had trouble restraining myself. But he did not want me to intervene. I knew he was able to take the ritual but I was his father and did want him to put up with any more than he had to.

We actually came closer together when he was initiated. The both of us being Omega, as well as my older son and nephew's intentions to one day complete their pledgeship, never interfered with our blood relationship. Communication seemed so much easier afterward. We seemed to have so much more in common. The whole area of trust seems to have improved. Once some other young people, boys and girls, were at our home and the matter of how my son decided to go Omega came up. He told them it was either go Omega or have to pay for it out of his own pocket. They all laughed heartily, for some of them had faced the same dilemma. But that was not the real reason he went Omega. He never told me, but he acted it. The reason he went Omega was because the men of Omega, including those he knew, tried to stand for something positive, something impressive and meaningful and that is why he chose to become a Que. A few weeks after he was initiated, and I could afford the money, I gave him a paddle saying that he was both a son and a brother.

Nearly four years later there was a newcomer to the family, my older son's little boy Phillip was born. His baby picture at three months old resting peacefully in my arms in dictates my hope for him. Perhaps he will see something in his father and his uncle, in his grandfather, which will encourage him to want to be like us in some small way. We will have to wait to see if he continues as a chip off the old block. We hope Omega Psi Phi Fraternity will be around to become one of the choices open to him.

March of the Generations 115

Brother Bryce Lawrence Morgan (1966-1986), to whom this memoir is dedicated.

Roosevelt Morgan and Georgia Madlock, about 1927. They were the parents of Thomas and Gordon Morgan. At the time of the shot he was about 20 and she about 17. His vehicle is in the left backgrounds. Our parents thought much of the principles of Omega, though they were not collegiate.

Brother Thomas Morgan, the author's blood brother, preceded him in joining the Fraternity in 1949 at Arkansas AM&N College, pine Bluff, Tau Sigma Chapter.

Brother Forrest Coleman and family. He is the youngest Omega member of the family.

Air Force Major Brian Morgan and wife Sherri (Delta Sigma Theta), Ashley and Phillip.

March of the Generations 119

Bro. James L. Wise.

Brother Walter R. Smith, Tau Sigma Chapter, Arkansas AM&N College, ca. 1951.

Brother Josh Criswell, Kansas State University, ca. 2007.

Brother Lonnie Ray Williams.

Addendum I

Tribute to Bro. Lonnie Ray Williams

The life of the fraternity is the initiation of new members. In the past this was the high point of emotion for the brothers and reunited them in their resolve to promote the values of the brotherhood. Some thought this to be their opportunity to see that the new brothers were properly initiated, to take into their own thoughts the meaning of the fraternity. Initiations provided opportunities for brothers to come together whose jobs and other activities often prohibited their seeing each other as regularly as they would hope. The variety which was found in any group of initiates was remarked upon for each new brother was indeed a unique personality seeking to be molded to the ideals of the fraternity. Each was expected to be able to contribute in his own special way.

Where there are enough men, young or not so young, wanting to be a part of what the fraternity represents, new chapters may be formed. Brothers' jobs may carry them to various towns and cities during their careers. If they are extremely enthusiastic about the fraternity, and are excited about what it may represent and teach, they may be on the leading edge of the establishment of new chapters.

In Northwest Arkansas, at the University of Arkansas, the author was credited with having founded Gamma Eta, the first black Greek chapter at the University. It received its charter in 1974 with the initiation of eleven new brothers.

One of these brothers was Lonnie Ray Williams. Brother Williams then was a leader among the initiates. He was a good student and exhibited achievement of the Cardinal Principles. He was adjustable enough to be considered for various positions of responsibility with the University structure, advancing from positions with the department of public safety to assistant dean of minority students. He was promoted in that position and at the present writing (mid-1990s) is Associate Vice Chancellor for Minority Affairs, with oversight of several units of University services.

Brother Williams can properly be said to be the virtual soul of Omega on the campus. He has had something to do with nearly all of the activities of the undergraduates, of whom he served as sponsor. Several years ago he was very instrumental in helping the area receive a graduate chapter, Upsilon Chi, of which he served as basileus. He has promoted membership in this chapter to involve areas not directly within the sphere of University influence. Members of the chapter are located as far as 90 miles away.

18

Back to the Beginning

My life as a Greek began after I entered the Agricultural and Normal College, Pine Bluff, Arkansas, after finishing as valedictorian of Pine Street School, Conway, Arkansas. That was a 1-12 school, meaning it housed all twelve grades in three buildings. One building housed most of the grades, a small building served as the home economics room and a third about 150 yards from the main building as a Smith-Hughes building which we called the Shop.

The teachers of the school were relatively new. The coach was a rather interesting man named Robert Williams who had come from North Carolina, they tell me. I never was sure. But Mr. Williams had more knowledge than anyone I had ever seen. He presented it well. I think he defended history. He had been rather activist in the community in the late1940s and had opened a community center in an abandoned pool hall. Williams left, as far as I remember, about 1948 before I graduated. I have not heard of him, or from him since. Mrs. Irene Stewart was the music teacher. She worked as hard as anybody to get us in shape to attend the state musical festival at Philander Smith College in Little Rock. I think we won some sort of recognition for doing R. Nathaniel Dett's "Listen to the Lambs," with the help of our most talented soprano, the late Sarah Allen, probably the best natural talent I had seen up to that time. We practiced hard for that performance. We did not have a bus and so could not make the trip to Pine Bluff where there would have been other opportunities to perform.

Mr. and Mrs. Eugene Landers were the real powers at the school. Landers had taken over the principalship from Mr. Preston Mattison who had run the school since its beginning in at least the early 1920s, when my own father was a young man. He had gone to school to Mattison in country schools. Somehow there was a shake-up in school politics in the city and the Superintendent B.A. Short, who had been in the job since before most people could remember, left and so did Mattison. Some say there was a scandal over money. Anyway, Landers became principal in 1947.

The shop teacher I remember was Theo Jones, a returning veteran, as were Landers and Williams. He had taken over from some other Smith-Hughes men who seemed to stay a year in the school then move on. Several of them eventually moved on to AM&N College's agricultural and shop departments. There was a man named Leon Cowans, a local man, who was perhaps the best overall teacher I had. He knew geometry, drafting, bricklaying, carpentry, and had answers you wouldn't believe. He claims to have done everything. He had lost two fingers on his left hand, I believe and claimed, half seriously and half jokingly, that the only thing he could not do better than other folks was to point the second finger on his left hand. Cowans was recognized at a master craftsman and teacher. He was an independent thinker and had some conflict with the principal, over what, I do not know. I found later that the principal was the only Greek on the faculty. He was Alpha Phi Alpha. There was no Greek focus in the town for there were very few college graduates. Since the school was the only place where college students or graduates might be used, and since the number of graduates was about half of the teaching force, there simply was not much Greek activity in the community.

The Masonic Lodge and Eastern Star took care of the social life of the town, if it were not covered by the churches, of which there were nine by 1949.

My brother preceded me in college by a year, he having matriculated in 1948. Then there was some identification with members from particular home towns, though age made a great difference in terms of associates. My brother knew several men from Conway who had entered the college. About four of them were veterans, having enrolled since the war ended. One was James Martin, a dapper little zoot suit wearing man who always wore shined shoes. Others were Robert Cummings and Thomas Givan, both standout halfbacks on the Golden Lion football team in the late 1940s. The brightest of the group, by common consensus, was Fred Balenton, a big lineman who majored in biology and was Alpha Kappa Mu, the counterpart of Phi Beta Kappa. And there was Harold Cowans, a major in biology, who was not a veteran, but who was a very sound student. Thomas, my brother, made average grades during his first year and was eligible to pledge a fraternity.

Omega Psi Phi had been the first fraternity brought to the campus, in 1946 (a date subject to some debate with the claim that 1943 was the correct date), at the insistence of President Lawrence A. Davis who had taken over the school outright in 1943. Thomas made some friends and became quite excited about receiving the recognition which came with membership in a prestigious social fraternity. Although the Omegas had been established in 1911 and incorporated in 1914 at Howard University, Washington, D.C., there had not been unanimous agreement that chapters should be established at schools in the South. Many of the black colleges were unrated, especially the state schools. The sororities had been more skittish about allowing chapters at such schools than the fraternities. But after the war it was hard to keep chapters from being established at schools which wanted them probably because so many of the candidates for initiation were former soldiers.

In those days there was great competition between groups to see which ones could name the most outstanding faculty members on the campus or active persons in the city. In Pine Bluff there was elation at the naming of noted civil rights lawyer W. Harold Flowers. Of course it helped the cause of the chapter to list as Omegas, or Ques as they were then and now called, the president of the college, Lawrence A. Davis; the director of guidance, the dean of men J. Beauregard Jones, the head of business administration Butler T. Henderson, the director of the music department Ariel M. Lovelace, Malvin E. Moore, Jr., head of the tailor department, and the head of the sociology department Tilman C. Cothran.

The Alphas claimed that they had very outstanding people as well and sometimes it was hard to get beyond the Greek symbols. They listed such luminaries as the head of the mechanic arts department, the most distinguished professor of history Elbert Tatum, the head of the history department Ray F. Russell and the agriculture department head S. Alexander Haley. Not to be overlooked were those who did not put much into the organizations. They were called lukewarm because of their low levels of enthusiasm or participation after their initiation. Others became almost new personalities. They lived for their Greek associations. They were the biggest supporters of their groups and often put their personal goals secondary to those of their fraternity or sorority.

They wore some insignia daily to identify their membership in their society. Such individuals saw going Greek as a sign of achievement of at least one of their goals in college. For some it was almost as important as getting a degree. It was not uncommon for students to come to college, get initiated into a group, then withdraw from school. That way they could still participate in all Greek activities but would not have to study for attainment of their degrees. Of course, there were other reasons for dropping out of school which had no relationship to Greek membership. There was fierce competition between the various Greek chapters on the campus.

One of the big activities was the Delta Sigma Theta Sorority Jabberwock, an annual program of 30 minute plays by surrounding schools and colleges. Students had to write their plays, get up the staging, and present them before audiences. They were graded by the staff members of the speech and drama department The groups making the finals were to present at a Saturday evening affair in the school auditorium. There were prizes given for winning. But the main incentive was to have your group win the Jabberwock. It meant much practice. One year our group won it. The play depicted the rise of totalitarianism in Europe and Russia, beginning with Adolf Hitler and ending with Joseph Stalin. The play had certain political implications of which we were not aware but, in retrospect, the writer, then a speech and drama major John M. Stevenson (Later Kilimanjaro) showed a good understanding of what was to come. He had rigged up a rather dangerous scene which called for Stalin to drop out of the ceiling and make a dramatic entry onto the stage of world affairs.

Serenading the campus was another activity we enjoyed. There were virtual sing-offs between the groups. The Omegas and the Alphas were the biggest competitors, though the Kappas and the Sigmas made runs from time to time. At first these serenades were spontaneous. There were two small cafes on the campus. Sometimes the brothers gathered there, quaffing a few cokes, eating hotdogs, and talking of their individual or group greatness. They would feel pretty pumped up and would leave the eating places headed for the dormitories singing. It was important to have great harmony for if there were disorganization and poor singing the group could be given thumbs down by those listening and would lose status on the campus.

Sometimes after an emotional meeting the group would spend some of its energy by serenading. The girls dormitories were the final destination of the serenades. When the girls heard the songs they usually came to the windows and looked out shrieking their satisfaction and calling for certain brothers to sing certain tunes. Once a girl became so emotional upon listening to an Omega serenade she fell out of a window about 6 feet from the ground. Luckily she was not hurt.

In those days the Greek societies were more social than service. E. Franklin Frazier had not published his famous *Black Bourgeoisie* and so we had not yet found how important Greek life was in black society. There were some efforts toward doing something for unfortunate persons in the community, but these were not the main focus of the organizations. Groups actually practiced their vocalizing during their meetings in order that through this means they might make a better impression on campus.

The groups sang their way around the quadrangle, their voices carrying for blocks in the still air of basically rural Pine Bluff. Serenading fraternities signaled that the students were not disturbed. The authorities of the campus could breathe a little easier when they heard the students serenading.

Through the fraternity I was able to knock off many of the rough edges I had coming from a country school in Conway, Arkansas. I got up my courage, gained confidence in myself, for I had a group behind me that was giving support.

I did not have much time after college to think about anything. I had decided to do my time in the Army and try after two years to get on with my life. I went to service less than a month after college, ending up in Korea in late 1953. I ran across very few Omegas there. There were not many college graduates who were black in the service in those days, or others either, who were enlisted. But one year in Korea I ran across Donald Mullett who later was a top administrator at Lincoln University in Pennsylvania and we had a Little Conclave. I wrote it up and it was printed in the *Oracle*.

Soon after military service it was back to school, this time graduate school at the University of Arkansas. There it seemed that the Ques were still seeking higher learning. George Wesley and John Stevenson (now Kilimanjaro) were in drama studying for master's degrees. Carl Brooks was trying to get certified in pharmacy.

We all suffered through our various classes. And there were Alphamen Ernest Dees and E. K. Blakely, Kappaman Professor Leonodis Barron, and non-Greek Homer Winstead on campus. There were some other students who did not mix too much with us and they evidently were not Greek. But there was no real emphasis on the symbols of Greekdom beyond a little kidding. We had very serious goals to reach and could not be distracted too much by frivolities.

By 1956 when I began teaching social sciences and mathematics at my old school, there still was no emphasis on Greekdom in my community. My future brother-in-law James Leroy Wise, later an important official in the regional leadership of the fraternity, and I did go to Little Rock where we affiliated for a time with Pi Omicron Graduate Chapter there. But even then it was hard to make the trip of 32 miles one way. The highway was very crooked and there were usually activities at our school which required our presence. There were activities in the Pine Bluff area which we could have attended but Pine Bluff was 45 miles beyond Little Rock which made that out of the question pretty nearly. It seemed that Greekdom was receding into the background as the raising of families and working daily took precedence over other obligations and interests.

In 1959 I was asked to take a post as an instructor of sociology at AM&N College, Pine Bluff. There was a graduate chapter there, Tau Phi. I became a member but found that there was a certain degree of structure in the Pine Bluff community which made it difficult for newcomers and persons without medical, law, dental, or doctoral degrees, and expensive houses to get accepted. As a brand new faculty member, holding the lowest rank, living in a very modest home, there was no way to gain recognition and respectability. The fraternity already had its structure, its leaders, its wheels, and cracking that nut would be hard. I did not know how long I would even be in Pine Bluff since I did not have tenure and evidently was not even on the tenure track. The emphasis then was on getting people who had doctoral degrees. I had only a master's and a few unrecognized hours beyond, not even enough to get me into the category of assistant professor at the college. If I wanted to survive in the ranks as a college teacher there were only two choices and those were to play politics or get a doctoral degree. I did not know anyone who was interested in me and so I had no political base. That left me no option but to go after the Ph.D.

But while I was in Pine Bluff I saw how the society was structured more clearly than I had ever imagined. The main thing that counted was not what one's Greek society was, or how many degrees he had, but what kind of house one lived in. The neighborhood was not so important in those days. Very few blacks of the middle class lived in white neighborhoods, though some did, having inherited property there from their parents. More commonly household help had acquired small houses in the white neighborhood. They would be entitled to remain there until they died or moved, then their homes would be demolished. In time the neighborhood would be converted to one for a single ethnicity. Black people were then thrown back upon their efforts to build beautiful homes in their sections of town. And some of them did. It was the quality of the house that made the difference. A man with no degrees and no Greek affiliation but who had a beautiful, well-appointed home, was higher in status than one who had a hind pocket full of degrees, Greek affiliation and living in a rented house.

19

Black Greek Life Today

Black fraternities and sororities are at a crossroads in their histories. They were begun largely out of reaction to the failure of majority Greek societies to include them during the Reconstruction Period when black students could attend majority colleges and when colleges were opened for them during the era of Jim Crow. Alpha Phi Alpha Fraternity was begun in 1905 at Cornell University. After its opening Howard University became a favorite institution at which black Greek societies were begun. Omega Psi Phi Fraternity, Kappa Alpha Psi, Delta Sigma Theta Sorority, and one or two others were begun at Howard.

At these institutions, although there was some copying of the behaviors of the older majority Greek societies, the situations at the black colleges were relatively different and so Greek life took on a different look at these colleges. An important feature was the influence they had on college life. Most of the life of the campus revolved around the Greek societies. They were almost as important as the athletic functions. It was through the Greek system that the balls and parties and social life revolved. A youth who was not Greek had a hard time maintaining a high profile on campus. Greek standing was a big help in promoting personal development, confidence, poise, leadership, and other socially desirable qualities. A qualitative difference was thought to have existed between Greeks and non-Greeks.

Initiation into the Greek society was a process that was taken very seriously by those seeking entry. The first was the maintaining of a grade point average high enough to differentiate one from the regular run of students. Generally something higher than a C+

was required by the college and often a B average was required by the chapter. A number of hours had to be accumulated such that freshmen were not eligible for admission, most generally.

The initiation period was generally about 8 weeks and not all societies were required to follow the same pledge period. Thus, some Greeks were on the pledge line a good deal of time of any semester. Two lines were not uncommon, but most societies had only one pledge line per school year.

Pledging was expected to teach a variety of values. The private part of the process was different from the public. Chapters met in rooms in buildings. There they quizzed pledges over aspects of the history of the organization and exacted mild punishments for their not knowing, or if they knew too much. A pledgee's being too "cocky" could yield as much "hazing" as one who knew too little. Paddling was not uncommon, but pledgees wore so much padding that very seldom did he or she feel any blow that was issued. Pledgees who did not want to take the paddling usually were dismissed from the pledge club. Deans of the college and advisors were very strict in the supervision of pledgees and greatly discouraged hazing. Advisors were usually younger faculty members of the organization who oversaw the activities of the pledgees and their leaders.

The public part of the process involved running throughout the campus, at any time of day or night, in the accomplishment of tasks such as polishing shoes, waking up of brothers in the morning, carrying books for a brother publicly, etc., were considered normal. Addressing Greeks properly was a duty that was looked forward to eagerly by both pledgees and initiated Greeks. Some service projects were undertaken to illustrate that the chapter was interested in more than fun and games. Pledgees were expected to keep up their grades and pledge activities were not to interfere with classwork. Occasionally, pledge work would take precedence over other extracurricular work a student was doing. If the pledge were a leader in another organization, while pledging the next level leader would take over. The last week of the period was thought of as "strict pledging." The pledge was not to talk to anyone unauthorized, and the final meal before initiation was to be a square one, meaning all movements involving spoons, knives, and forks were to be conducted at right angles.

The pledge group became tightly bonded and became the nucleus of the later center of the chapter. Often the pledge club had to make a public appearance, such as going to church as a group where they would be recognized by the congregation. Moving from neophyte to full member was greatly anticipated. One was not a full Greek until he or she had participated in the initiation of another group.

When the initiation was finished there was a great emotional outpouring by the new members, and campus individuals who had been observing them during their pledge period. The ceremony was conducted with great intensity and sincerity and affected other students as well who resolved to get their grades up so they could pledge. There were some variations from chapter to chapter and from group to group, but this practice was common enough.

Today, well over half of black Greek chapters are located on majority white campuses. The conditions have changed. Where black Greeks were special on black campuses, they are not on majority campuses. They still have the image of pledging that their parents and relatives instilled in them, but those practices cannot be carried out on the majority campuses, for the most part. A gap exists between what black Greek aspirants want and what their schools and national chapters will allow as these chapters reflect the rules and regulations of the respective campuses. The problem is similar to that which existed when Native Americans were confined to reservations where it became more difficult to carry out their former rituals, especially those involving the buffalo. The majority campus is like a reservation for black students. It is not their campus and they cannot behave as they could on their own campus. Black campuses likewise have changed so that they are like majority campuses and students must act as they do on majority campuses. With respect to Greek life, they must operate under many more restrictions than when they were mostly confined to black campuses. The culture of those campuses developed holistically—activities operated together and seldom were in conflict.

A big difference between becoming Greek today and yesterday is cost. The cost to the present writer was $30, 57 years ago. The cost today is about $600. The process is much different. There is not the public observation of the pledging process. The emotion is taken out of the process and so are teaching and bonding of members.

The Omega Psi Phi Fraternity, Incorporated:

A Script

The black Greek Movement began in America soon after the Plessy Decision of 1896, which legalized separation of the races. Prior to that time a few blacks had become members of the old line Greek letter groups such as Phi Beta Kappa. These groups were more academic than social then, but as they expanded, they became more social creating difficulties for blacks who were generally being rejected for social life.

The Sigma Phi Boulé, was the first of the black Greek letter societies. It was not college based and was made up of promising members of black society who thought that it was their role to lead the others toward first class citizenship.

It was at Cornell University, in Ithaca, New York, in 1906, that the first black collegiate Greek letter society, Alpha Phi Alpha, was founded. It was a response to rejection. Cornell had been a leading school from which blacks were willing to study and receive their advanced degrees. As a member if the Ivy League, it had great prestige. Its Department of Agriculture was especially appealing to black students who would return to the South and serve as instructors to the freedmen and their offspring.

Howard University, in Washington, D.C., had been the leading school for blacks in the East. Howard was considered the elite black college and parents wanted their children to go there for study. From Howard they could have the literal pick of the schools at which they may teach, and they could also find work in the Federal Government. It was predictable that Howard University would be the venue for the development of the black Greek system.

Around 1910, or soon after the Alphas were established at Cornell, Howard students and faculty began their own societies.

They operated long before they were incorporated. Omega Psi Phi, for example, had operated openly since 1911, but was not incorporated until 1914. Other schools where blacks were enrolled in significant numbers began campaigns for their own societies. At Indiana University, Kappa Alpha Psi was founded, around 1914.

Female counterparts of these organizations were founded around the same time as their male counterparts. Delta Sigma Theta was founded around the time of the founding of Omega Psi Phi. Zeta Phi Beta and Phi Beta Sigma were founded and made arrangements that they would present themselves as collegiate sisters and brothers. Other pairings became a part of social expectations, even though they were not formal. Alpha Phi Alpha and Alpha Kappa Alpha enjoyed loose arrangements of sisterhood and brotherhood. Sigma Gamma Rho and Kappa Alpha Psi were joined, though not as closely as some of the others.

Social life on the campuses where these societies were located revolved around them. Nearly all students wanted to become members of whatever Greek societies as were prominent on their campuses. This led to a certain amount of contentiousness among the students for bids to enter the societies. The blackball was thought to be a favorite method of limiting membership. Nor did the associations need to give any reasons why a person was not accepted. The fees were a limitation for many of the students at the colleges were not affluent. Nor did their parents think that membership in the organizations was crucial.

Aside from the prestige that accrued, especially locally, the Greek letter membership held steady, and on some campuses increased. A chapter of 30 members was thought to be large. Most probably averaged between 10 and 20 members, replacing these with one-time initiations of seldom more than five or six per year. A dozen initiates in some societies, especially among the females, was relatively uncommon.

This program is largely about Omega Psi Phi Fraternity, begun at Howard University in 1911. Its founders were three undergraduates and one faculty member.

Show Oscar J. Cooper, Ernest Just, Frank Coleman. Edgar A Love, was the faculty member. These men later achieved distinction in their fields, especially Ernest Just, an internationally known chemist. Edgar A. Love was a very distinguished churchman.

The principles upon which the fraternity was founded were Manhood, Scholarship, Perseverance and Uplift. The intent was to promote these values so as to produce very well rounded young men. The candidate for initiation was to exhibit high potential for reaching each of these principles.

All the societies had similar principles as their goals, even though they may have utilized other names. Since they were the dominant social societies in the black community, they were in something of a competitive struggle, even though they worked together to put over various programs and undertakings. When all the Greeks cooperated they could accomplish what the other organizations in the city or area could not. For that reason nearly all the young people with upward mobility and black improvement as their goals, wanted to join the Greek societies.

After a history of Greekdom was achieved, parents who were Greek wanted their children to be legacies, to follow them into their societies. (Show pictures of fathers and son; mothers and daughters, grandparents, etc.).

Work in the fraternity or sorority could have payoffs in the community. In Washington, D.C., Federal Government was keen to assure that the representatives of the black Greek system were incorporated at high levels. H. Carl Moultrie translated the Executive Secretaryship of Omega Psi Phi Fraternity into a Federal Judgeship.

Most of the programs at the many black colleges that were in the South utilized the most recognizable blacks as their speakers. Almost inevitably they utilized persons trained at the collegiate level. Since most of these persons had received some, if not all of their training at black colleges, they were members of Greek letter societies, for the most part. Students used the Greek association of the speakers to their advantage. A favorite pastime among students at these colleges was to compare what persons were most achieving in their associations, on a national basis, with those in other groups.

The Omegas were proud to mention a large number of men of achievement, such as Ralph Bunche, Judge William Hastie, Carter G. Woodson, Benjamin E. Mays, literally dozens of college presidents, military officers, medical doctors, lawyers (Wiley E. Branton), scholars, etc. (Show their pictures).

Houses: When the black Greek movement started, there was the idea that chapter houses were important. They symbolized the intent to separate from the larger student body in a promotion of exclusiveness. It was thought that with students working together as a brotherhood in separate environments, they would serve as more positive role models for the other students thereby encouraging their own achievement.

Houses were expensive. Substitutes had to be found. In some schools wings in dormitories were adopted for certain organizations. These were never formal, but in some cases a wing could be noted as the Alpha Wing, the Kappa Wing, the Sigma Wing, or the Omega Wing. It was similar in regards to the sororities. In some cases, where students lived off campus, several members of the same fraternity roomed together and that house became known as the house of a particular fraternity.

Over time, it was found that the house was not the central identity feature of the Greek association. It was what the members stood for and how they acted. Remaining identified with the student body by living in the same dormitories as the non-Greeks, allowed the Greeks to show that they were indeed better role models. They interacted with the non-Greeks at such a common level that they would attract students to their organization for reasons other than materialism. Moreover, the money that was accumulated at the national level need not be used for the maintenance of real estate, but could be used for scholarships and other services.

The Oracle

The chief organ of the fraternity is the *Oracle*, published quarterly. It carries materials that announce the achievements of the brothers. Since the fraternity is organized in terms of regions or districts, some space is devoted to each of these twelve districts and to international chapters-Social Affairs: The idea that community development can be carried on within a social context has been well known by the black Greeks. In the cities there is considerable competition to see which group can put on the most successful social affairs. These are usually big dances or cotillions. Debutante balls were sponsored by the fraternities for the purpose of introducing young women to society. Since this is a principal way of becoming introduced to society, and girls must meet high standards, the impact is strong and encourages both young ladies and young men to meet those standards. (Show Alpha Phi Alpha Debutante Ball Pictures.) They become fairly well expected in almost any city. Howard University, for years had a Kappa Alpha Psi Boat Ride that was the social event of the community. The Omega Ball was usually a big affair requiring extensive hotel accommodations. The ball at the National Conclave was attended by nearly all who were trying to work in community improvement. To get snubbed from participation in these social events is disturbing to some individuals for this event is one of the occasions in which they may assert themselves in a wider social context. In earlier days, the balls were associated with colleges, but latterly, they moved off campus. Nearly all the organizations use extra funds from these affairs for scholarships.

It was the sociologist E. Franklin Frazier who noted in the early 1940s that black society revolved around activities that all had the character of fraternities, whether they were in civil rights, education, or religious work. The Greek letter societies were very prominent and their members usually dominated in this work.

Although much has changed, much has remained practically unchanged. The factors that promoted the growth of black Greek letter societies over 100 years ago are still present. A youth in college, wanting to promote community life through associations would do well to join a Greek letter society. These societies are now integrated and some majority students enjoy membership in them and adopt their teachings and programs.

Chapters

There are three types of chapters in the fraternity. They are: Undergraduate, Intermediate, and Graduate. The undergraduate chapter requirements are set in part by the school and by the national body. In some schools a 2.00 average on a 4 point scale is required. In others it will be higher. A student must be properly enrolled in a college in order to pledge the fraternity. Ordinarily a number of hours are required before pledging. Because there are many factors that determine whether a student remains in college, the Intermediate chapter has been established. It is made up in towns or cities of persons who have attended college, who pledged the fraternity, but have not graduated. The Graduate chapter is made up of men who have graduated from college.

These chapters also serve to allow the interests of brothers to operate according to age and rank. It is well known that younger brothers have different interests than older brothers. So the graduate chapters are usually composed of older, more mature brothers. A brother can find a chapter regardless of his collegiate status.

Fellowship

It was the feeling of fellowship and brotherhood that attracted young men to these associations. The Omegas were known for their sense of brotherhood that lasted throughout life. That is one thing that binds these brothers together no matter how different they may be on the surface.

Show pictures of some prominent Ques

Corliss Williamson, Michael Jordan, Jesse Jackson, Bill Cosby, Lawrence A. Davis, Astronauts, Scholars like Benjamin E. Mays.

Hymn

Show Omegas singing Hymn.

End

Addendum II

Will My Son Pledge Omega?

Don't let my boy go Alpha
A dying mother said.
Don't let my boy go Kappa
I'd rather see him dead.

Don't let my boy go Sigma
It's just a club you see
But let him go Omega
It's the only fraternity.

It was nearly 30 years ago that I first heard this song in pledge club meetings at AM&N College, now the University of Arkansas at Pine Bluff. By then it had been sung many years in the chapters of Omega at campuses across the country. At that time the meaning of the poem/song did not extend much farther than getting back at the other Greek organizations with which the Omegas competed. There were some second generation Ques, but not many, for the fraternity was relatively young and two generations of black college men from the same family were relatively rare. Seldom could a black youth in college say his father was a college man.

The greater access of black Americans to colleges within the past century or so has meant sons can now say somewhat more frequently that their fathers were college men. The case was dramatized to me a few years ago at the Houston Conclave when many Omega extended families were in attendance.

Today, many Omega men, all of whom believe in the merits of higher education, face the problem of whether their sons will pledge Omega. Naturally, they hope they will. The words of one brother are illustrative. He said one thing would surely break his heart and that would be the failure of his sons to join Omega Psi Phi. This brother's words indicate his love for and commitment to the ideals of the fraternity.

Probably when the opening poem was written, black fathers could not often encourage their sons to follow in their footsteps. Masonic lodges were perhaps the only social organizations in which fathers could be honored in seeing their sons take up membership.

But what are the issues underlying the problems of sons joining their fathers' fraternities? At one level fathers may feel that sons should make their own fraternal choices, just as they made theirs a generation or more ago. Would an Omega father and an Alpha son really be the end of the world? Indeed some sons may not join any fraternity feeling they don't mean as much as they did to their fathers. Newer generations have emerged, black youth have scattered to many different campuses and black Sigma Chi's and Kappa Sig's are not unheard of.

A number of fathers may pledge not to help sons with fees and expenses if they do not join their organizations. Enmity may be created when father and son cannot agree on the son's fraternal choices. There is no easy answer to the issue posed. Perhaps each father and son will have to solve it in their own way. What we can say is that as a concept of human brotherhood there is none better or more salient than Omega Psi Phi Fraternity. The principles for which the fraternity stands translate into human decency of the highest order. If Omega has men in its ranks that try to live by such principles it shows the principles mean something to the men. Meaning carries over into action and this is the reason any community knows that an Omega man is present.

Sons learn from their fathers and every Omega man with a son has an obligation to train him in the basic principles of humanism. If he does a good job the son will see what Omega means and the choice for him to join, when he is eligible, will not be a difficult one.

Every child does not make choices which satisfy its parents. Some select the wrong schools, careers, friends, or marriage partners. It requires parental open-mindedness to accept their choices. When a parent has done all that is reasonable to discourage a poor choice, or to encourage a good one, what more can be done?

It must be realized that, while children and their parents are much alike, they are not exactly alike. Each remains a fundamentally different person. Concerning Omega Psi Phi, it is good enough for father and, hopefully, for sons. If, however, the son doesn't make that choice, well, "different strokes for different folks."

From the *Oracle*, published in Spring of 1997
By Gordon D. Morgan, Ph.D.
Professor of Sociology
University of Arkansas
Fayetteville, Arkansas

www.ingramcontent.com/pod-product-compliance
Lightning Source LLC
Chambersburg PA
CBHW031643170426
43195CB00035B/508